G. de Molinari, Walter K. Firminger

Religion

G. de Molinari, Walter K. Firminger

Religion

ISBN/EAN: 9783337131197

Printed in Europe, USA, Canada, Australia, Japan

Cover: Foto ©Lupo / pixelio.de

More available books at **www.hansebooks.com**

"PHILOSOPHY AT HOME" SERIES.

RELIGION

BY

G. DE MOLINARI

CORRESPONDANT DE L'INSTITUT

RÉDACTEUR EN CHEF "DU JOURNAL DES ECONOMISTES

TRANSLATED FROM THE SECOND (ENLARGED) EDITION
WITH THE AUTHOR'S SANCTION

BY

WALTER K. FIRMINGER B.A.

MERTON COLLEGE, OXFORD

LONDON
SWAN SONNENSCHEIN & CO.
NEW YORK: MACMILLAN & CO.
1894

59803

To

H. SCOTT HOLLAND, M.A.

CANON AND PRECENTOR OF

ST. PAUL'S CATHEDRAL

LATE STUDENT OF CHRIST CHURCH, OXFORD

THIS TRANSLATION IS

(BY KIND PERMISSION)

RESPECTFULLY DEDICATED.

INTRODUCTION.

———oo҉ೲ҉oo———

THE aim of this little volume is to establish on a scientific basis the claim of the Christian Church to an equitable treat- ment on the part of not only its opponents, but even its habitual supporters. The translator feels that nothing he could say in this place would in reality add to the tenor of M. de Molinari's vigorous statement. There are indeed many points on which the translator's views would harshly contrast with those of his author. Yet the serious purpose of the work and its clear enunciation of many fundamental problems (such, for instance, as the admirable chapters dealing with the relations of Science and Religion, and the existing obstacles to the movement for establishing the Church's freedom), seem to justify the translator in the task he has so unworthily fulfilled.

In his treatment of the rise of early religions, and of Christi- anity in particular, M. de Molinari has no doubt laid too much stress on subjective elements. Christianity may be explained by many analogies ; it indeed, to some extent, bases its claim on an interpretation of man's nature ; but Christianity taught before it explained, and we must be careful not to fall into the inviting *post hoc ergo propter hoc* fallacy.

M. de Molinari's book is, of course, a plea for Disestablish- ment, but hardly in the sense of the Liberation Society. In England there are, roughly speaking, three parties who claim great expectations in a measure so dreaded by Conservatives. The Secularist would disestablish and disendow in the interests of a so-called humanitarian policy ; the Political Dissenter takes his stand on a not very intelligible plea for religious equality.

b

Churchmen on the extreme left of the Catholic Movement desire by such a step to secure liberty for a State-ridden Church. Disestablishment now appears as inevitable ; the question only remains—with which of these three parties the drafting of the measure will lie. The schemes of the Secularist, we feel confident, will no more commend themselves to the Englishman's sense of reverence than the schemes of the Political Nonconformist will commend themselves to his sense of justice. The Liberation Society has only to draft its bill in order to throw back for years a measure which can but provoke popular disgust. For, as M. de Molinari sums up the matter, " The necessary condition of religious progress is the separation of Church and State, effected not in hostility to, but in favour of religion."

But will the extreme left of the " High-Church Party" carry the day ? Will the "Nonconformist conscience" consent to allow "sacerdotalism to run rampant?" To this question M. de Molinari will supply us with an unanswerable reply. If the Nonconformists are so afraid of "sacerdotalism " as to wish to place legal restrictions on its progress, all we can say is that their angry demand for religious freedom and the removal of State distinction is intensely one-sided. It is the Nonconformist, not the Churchman, who has most to fear from " Religious Equality." [1]

If, however, Churchmen wish to forestall Disestablishment and Disendowment, they must be up and doing. The time for magic-lantern lectures on Church History is over ; the fact of the continuity of the modern English Church with the Church of Augustine, Aidan, Theodore, Dunstan, Becket, Wolsey, Warham, and Pole cannot now be seriously disputed. The present need is not so much a correction of fallacies, or a removal of prejudices, but rather an aggressive policy unanimously carried out. Neither is the matter so complex or so difficult as would be supposed. The legal documents which bind down the free voice of Convocation are but few, and nothing could be desired which would tend to bring more discredit on the policy of the Liberationist party than a refusal on their part to co-operate with the Church in a policy of Church emancipa-

[1] *Cf.* Note on pp. 144-5.

tion. Here then is a step which may easily be taken, and it is only just that it should be taken. Parliamentary Disestablishment would most certainly necessitate a certain amount of ecclesiastical reconstruction. Why should not the Church be charged with this duty—a duty which she alone can adequately accomplish? Why should we step out of one State prison to be enclosed in another?

The claim of each individual on the attention of the Church is not dependent on the Church's Nationality, but on its Catholicity. This last prerogative no State enactment can destroy. We need not therefore fear Disestablishment on this score, but this consideration will, however, suffice to put us on our guard against those syncretic schemes of "re-union," the ideal National Church theory about which we have of late heard so much. Nothing can be gained by allowing the Church's intensity to simmer down into an insipid diffusiveness. M. de Molinari in various parts has dealt the theological-debating-society ideal of a National Church some hard blows. Such a Church of compromise could but be "the sovereign pattern and exemplar of management, of the triumph of the political method in spiritual things, and the subordination of ideas to the *status quo.*"[1] We know the kind of man such a system must always tend to produce—"the safe man who can set down half a dozen general propositions which escape from destroying one another only by being diluted down into truisms"—the man whom the Church is said to want, "not party men, but sensible, temperate and sober, well-judging persons, to guide it through the channel of no meaning, between the Scylla and Charybdis of Aye and No."[1] The age, on the contrary, requires that a Church will satisfy, and not merely repeat its needs; a Church that will teach and not debate.

The first edition of M. de Molinari's work did not contain the second part which deals more exclusively with the present and future of religions. In order to render the present translation capable of appearing in the "Philosophy at Home Series," it was found necessary to omit the recapitulatory chapter which com-

[1] John Morley. *On Compromise,* p. 40.
[2] Cardinal Newman. *Essays, Critical and Historical,* vol. i., p. 301.

mences M. de Molinari's additional matter, and to indicate in footnotes the sources, rather than to quote at length the long catena of authorities published in the appendix to the French edition.

The translator has to thank his friends, Mr. G. F. Hill, B.A., of Merton College, Oxford, and the British Museum, and Mr. A. G. Nash of Exeter College, Oxford, for kindly reading through his proofs.

WALTER K. FIRMINGER.

St. Stephen's House, Oxford,
December, 1893.

AUTHOR'S PREFACE

→❋←

THE Radical and Socialist schools are, for the most part, anti-religious. In their eyes, all religions are superstitions, about which modern science has said the last word; they are the offspring of deception and credulity, and they have been in every age the instruments of oppression, robbery, and gross-ness. If, despite the progress of enlightenment, they continue to exist, it will be principally if not entirely due to the material conceded them by the State, whose subsidies and privileges they possess. But when they are brought under the control of common rights, their rights of property once and for all restricted, and the teaching by which they weaken and corrupt the spirit of the rising generation interdicted, they will speedily die of inanition. This is why the sup-pression of State support and the separation of Church and State figure in all the programmes of the Radical and Socialist schools and parties. But it is curious to observe that the Conservative classes, who are convinced that religion is imperishable, and who, with good reason, regard it as a necessary agent of civilisation, seem to agree in one respect with those who wish to destroy it—in the notion that the existence of religion is dependent upon its union with the State, and that it would be exposed to decay, if not to ex-tinction, should disestablishment come about and religion be reduced to existing on its own internal resources. The same classes regard difference of opinion in religious matters with open repugnance. For a long time they have been busy in reconstructing religious monopoly, and they con-tinue to regard the privileges, and, above all, the signature of the budget, as indispensable to the maintenance and the prosperity of religion. This is why they wish to preserve the subsidisation of the religious bodies, and are absolutely hostile to the separation of Church and State.

When, however, without party bias, we study the past of religion, we are irresistibly brought to recognise that religion is the offspring of a universal aspiration, that it is in consequence indestructible, that the progress of science, so far from destroying it, rather contributes to elevate, purify, and strengthen it that it has from the very first rendered possible the establishment of order and of the customs and laws which assure its existence, and without which society would not have been able to survive a civilisation to be born. The same study demonstrates that all religions, like all other manifestations of the human mind, have developed themselves and been made prosperous by the independence and liberty, that they have declined and become bankrupt under the *régime* of privilege and monopoly, that their action has been especially beneficent under the *régime* of competition. From this we may be permitted to conclude that the separation of Church and State, demanded by the Radicals and Socialists, and resented by the Conservatives as detrimental to religion, would, on the contrary, result in its extension and progress.

This, then, is the truth which we propose to place clearly before our readers. This book is a plea in favour of the independence and liberty of creeds. To all appearances such an attempt will minister to the taste of neither the enemies of religion nor its habitual defenders, for it will run counter to the prejudices of either party. Yet it has seemed to us that, at the present moment, in the dangerous crisis through which civilised societies are now passing, religion is more than ever a necessary agent of order and progress, and that it is therefore all the more necessary to show under what conditions it is able most efficaciously to exert its influence upon the conduct of individuals and the direction of human affairs.

CONTENTS

———∘∘⟨⊙⟩∘∘———

PART I.

THE PAST AND PRESENT OF RELIGIONS.

PART II.

THE FUTURE OF RELIGION.

PART I.

THE PAST AND PRESENT OF
RELIGIONS.

A

CHAPTER I.

THE RELIGIOUS INSTINCT—THE RELIGIONS OF THE
FIRST AGE OF HUMANITY.

RELIGION answers to an aspiration manifested in all ages and by every variety of the human species. As far as it is susceptible of analysis, it is an aspiration at once intellectual and moral. The natural instinct of the intelligence is to make itself acquainted with the causes of the phenomena of the senses. The natural instinct of the feelings is to love those things and beings which cause a sensation of pleasure, and to shun those which cause an impression of pain.[1] By picturing to ourselves the situation of the primitive man in the unknown environment into which he found himself cast, we shall make clear how these natural instincts of the intellectual and moral side of man's being have brought him to an embryonic conception of a religion. Not only was he exposed to the deadly attacks of the beasts with whom he had to struggle for subsistence, but his life was incessantly menaced by a host of baneful circumstances, earthquakes, floods, extremes of heat and cold, plagues.

[1] *Cf.* Darwin : *Descent of Man*, chap. ii. [The position assumed in this chapter is admirably discussed by the Rev. T. Strong in his admirable *Manual of Theology*.]

3

Other circumstances, such as the light and heat of the
sun, or of the fire which warmed and made his food
more tasteful would, on the other hand, produce in
him experiences of happiness. Would not these
occurrences which affected him for good or for
evil, and which acted thus despite himself, compel
him to attribute their existence to certain beings,
having like himself, though in a much higher degree,
the power of acting upon nature ?

These beings, endowed with a power superior to
his own, since they brought about occurrences he was
powerless to affect, the primitive man was led by a
particular faculty of his intellect, the imagination, to
picture to himself under a certain form suited to
their actions. He found, in this direction, certain
natural indications in his own constitution, and in
that of the other creatures according to the character
and imprints their passions had stamped on them. With
these materials he was able to create the idea of
powers good or evil, attributing to them either a
human shape, with an expression good-natured or
malicious, fair or cruel, or else the shape of a beast, or
of a vegetable noxious or useful, or indeed, of a rock
abrupt and threatening. To this idea men gifted
with some plastic talent gave a body, reproducing it
in some material they had at hand ; in potter's clay,
in wood, in stone, or in metal, according to the progress of their craftmanship. If the idol answered to
the idea the rest of the tribe had made for themselves of the power the idol was supposed to represent, they identified it with that power and loved
or dreaded it.

This phenomenon of the identification of an immaterial with a material object, in which it is embodied, is to be met with not only in the savage, who is the survival of the primitive man, but also in the lower strata of our civilised societies. Does not an analogous phenomenon present itself in the nature of children of the female sex under the excitement of maternal sentiment? The doll! such is the idol to which this sentiment at its embryonic stage has also given birth amongst every people. The doll is not a simple toy. It is a creature to whom the child attributes a spirit, desires, passions like her own, which she loves, cherishes, caresses, scolds, punishes and recompenses. ·The only difference existing between this idol of maternal sentiment, and the idol of religious sentiment is that the former embodies a fictitious obedient being who has a longing for care and protection, while the latter, on the contrary, embodies a being superior in power, a master instead of a pupil. But the force which animates the doll in the mind of the child, and the idol in the mind of the child-man of primitive times—is it not the same in either case?

It was, however, necessary to propitiate this immaterial power which the imagination embodied in an idol, in order either to obtain the good things which it was in its power to bestow, or to escape the evils it was in its power to inflict. Here, again, the primitive man had for his guidance the operations which had exercised an influence on himself, and which he employed in his dealings with fellow-beings. He had had many occasions to test the efficacy of prayer, and especially of presents offered in exchange for some favour or coveted possession. He addressed, then, his prayers to the idols in which were embodied the spirits in possession of powers superior to his own, and if his prayers were of no avail, he supplemented them by appropriate offerings.

Such is the first stage of the religious idea. It is fetichism or idolatry. But the instinct to which the idol or fetich answers does not necessarily imply a cult. It exists in our own times among backward folks who do not possess any cult, or maintain any priest, but are well satisfied with cherishing the religious life in their own homes.[1] The explanation of this fact is very simple, and it is the duty of political economy to supply it. It is to be found in the insufficiency of industrial production among backward folks ; these folks are too poor to maintain a priesthood ; they do not possess any priests for the same reason that painters and musicians are not found among them. Each individual performs his religious duties ; the artists and other persons of whose services they feel the need belong to the stage when quest of subsistence and self-defence do not absorb all man's time and activity.

It is only when a tribe or a people has commenced to develop its primitive industry, when it has invented the weapons which render the chase more profitable and self-defence more sure, that its members are able to economise a part of the time necessary for the production of indispensable articles and the preservation

[1] See De Quatrefages : *Introduction a l'Etude des Races Humaines*, pp. 235-66.

of their physical life. Instead of devoting the whole of their time, perhaps twelve hours per day, to the production of sustenance, they would not employ more than ten hours. This saved time they would be able either to spend in idleness or to use in satisfying the less urgent needs which until now had remained unsatisfied. But the more intelligent among them would not be slow to perceive that if they continued to employ the whole of their time in the production of means of subsistence, and so procure for themselves, by the exchange of their over-supply, the products or the services adapted to the satisfaction of their lesser wants, they would realise a new economy, and would be able to obtain the products or services in a greater quantity and superior quality in exchange for a smaller sum of industry and trouble. The advantage which they drew from this indirect production by means of the division of labour and of exchange becomes particularly clear when reference is made to the services demanding the talents and special knowledge of an order higher than the ordinary level.

The division of labour, however, can only operate through successive and gentle gradations. The industries which separate themselves from the common stem are afterwards, in default of an opening for each, combined by the same individual ; thus it is that in a village the same artisan executes the tasks of the carpenter and joiner, of decorator and painter, the grocer supplies articles of nutriment, tools, dresses, and eatables. Among a people whose industry is also in an elementary stage, the division of labour is, à fortiori, less complete. It commences commonly with a magician,

who at one and the same time fulfils the functions of
priest, doctor, law-giver, judge, and artist. The
magician may doubtless be ignorant, but his ignorance is less than that of his patrons. By observation
and experience, he acquires certain pieces of knowledge which they do not possess, and these pieces of
knowledge go on accumulating by a practice which
is often hereditary. The negro magician possesses a
whole body of useful notions. He knows the signs
which announce rain or dryness; he has discovered
the herbs which possess curative virtues; above all,
he has studied the character and chief inclinations of
his patrons, and he excels in rendering them the services which they demand. These services, it may be,
are clumsy; but they answer to needs which were
never, or, at the best, but imperfectly satisfied
before. The existence of the magician attests,
then, a realised progress, a step in the road of civilisation.

Thus, in the first phase of the life of humanity,
when it is still composed solely of herds of human
beings or tribes, living by hunting and the natural
fruits of the earth, the religious aspiration is satisfied at first by the very same individuals who themselves feel the want. Then, when the production
of means of subsistence has become sufficiently adequate to make a beginning of the division of labour,
there appears an intermediary, a magician, who
combines the medical and other services with those
adapted to satisfy the religious aspiration of the tribe.
Each tribe living in isolation, and usually in a state
of hostility with the neighbouring tribes, creates its own

religion, has its own idols, its own fetiches. Religion is thus in a rudimentary state, and so long as the resources of the tribe are limited by the insufficiency of its protective power and industry, only capable of a slight development.

CHAPTER II.

RELIGIOUS progress has been the result of economic advances, enabling the population of hunters, the tribes or clans of the primitive era, to multiply their numbers and increase their means of subsistence. As long as men have been reduced to live on the captures of the chase and the gleanings of unculti-vated fruits of the soil, a space of no more than six square miles was necessary to furnish food for a single individual, and these primitive indus-tries were so meagrely productive that the primi-tive man was obliged, as is the savage in our own times, to employ the greatest portion of his time in the search of sustenance. The discovery of alimentary plants, and the invention of agricultural tools, oc-casioned, in this state of existence, a double revolu-tion. On the one hand, the six square miles, which with difficulty sufficed to feed a single hunter, were now able with equal success to maintain a thousand agriculturalists; while, on the other hand, our thou-sand agriculturalists are now able to produce this supply of sustenance by employing, instead of the whole, only half their time; or, what comes to the

10

same thing, five hundred agriculturalists, employing
the whole of their time in the production of food,
produce sufficient sustenance to maintain a thousand
individuals. The better half, then, of the population
are, in consequence, able to devote themselves to the
industries or professions providing for the physical or
moral wants, which they had hitherto been able
to satisfy but imperfectly, if at all. The industrial tribes, however, who had realised this
decided progress, and whose population had thus
acquired an extraordinary extent, were, continually
threatened with destruction by tribes of hunters
and cannibals, less advanced, but more war-
like. As we have remarked elsewhere, this went on
until the time when these men of prey, perceiving
that the regular exploitation of industrious men would
repay them better than pillage, transformed themselves from brigands and plunderers into police.[1]
They permanently established themselves in the territories they had previously been content to lay waste,
and reduced to slavery instead of massacring the
population, who were rendered incapable of self-defence
by the very nature of their mode of life. Slavery, there
fore, was, to consider its better side, the first means of
security. Beyond all doubt, cost of the assurance was
a lion's share. The insurer himself fixed the premium,
and from the very first he did not fail to set at the
maximum the quantity of labour which his protection
enabled him to demand in return. But if this
premium was expensive, it remained smaller than the

[1] Molinari : *Notions Fundamentales d'Economie Politique,*
Introduction.

risk of destruction it averted. Protected permanently
against pillage and destruction, the industrial population will multiply and continuously augment their
production. Now vast and populous States will
shelter a population numerous, and abundantly provided with the necessities of life, on territories where,
until now, some hundreds of hunters found with difficulty the means of existence.

The interval between the gross religions of the folks
who live miserably by the chase and the natural fruits of
the soil, and the religions of the nations who have constituted themselves, and who, thanks to the advance
in systematic agriculture and the security in production under the primitive form of slavery, have increased in numbers or in wealth—the interval between
the religions of the first stage and the second stage of
humanity is considerable.   Like all other kinds of
progress, religious progress is accomplished when
there is a demand for progress, and this demand was
produced as soon as the conception of the first age had
ceased to satisfy the peoples who had arrived at a certain
degree of civilisation, such as had been attained by the
states, empires, kingdoms, or simple cities of Egypt,
Assyria, of India, of China, and later of Greece and Italy.
In the bosom of these nations on the road to civilisation,
the performers of religious services not only increased
in numbers but split themselves up into classes. and
castes, varying in intelligence and culture.   Whereas
in the primitive folk the generality of intelligence
remained at the same level, determined by the purely
material character of the search for sustenance, it was
no longer so in the nations of the second age.   If the

state of the inferior stage of society had been entirely expressed by a multitude of tasks demanding almost exclusively the application of physical force, and by this very fact the development of the intellectual faculties had been stunted; there was another and a superior kind of needs which evoked the employment of superior faculties—the governing functions of the State, of the city, of the family, the fine arts, commerce, etc. The childish ideas and inventions of the tribal magicians, the embodiment of spirits in rude idols, the fetiches, amulets, which till now satisfied the religious wants of the masses bound to the toil of beasts of burden, no longer suited the higher classes, nor, indeed, the middle classes, whose duties and occupations exacted in different degrees an intelligent co-operation of the intelligence and moral faculties. Society then appealed to the descendants of the magician for a religion less rude. This religion it conceived and invented by preserving the primitive cult which it had received as a heritage, and transforming it after the model before its eyes of the political and economic organism—a model which had come into existence under the influence of the advance in regular culture of the soil.

This religious concept is characterised by the consecration of the State or city to its gods, the division of labour or the specialisation of the attributes and functions of the deities, the constitution of a divine and hierarchical government, in harmony with the new conditions of society. The divine organisation is clearly based on the economic organisation of the societies of the second age; the gods are impelled

by the human motive power of self-interest; the
sentiments and passions which animate them are
those which are stamped on human nature.

I. *The consecration of the State to its gods.*—It
must not be forgotten that until quite recently our
ideas of the universe were singularly narrow. In the
eyes of the ancients our globe was by itself the whole
of the universe. They pictured it as an immense
plain broken by mountains and shut in by the ocean.
Above it circled the unbroken vault of heaven, from
which were suspended. the lamps of the sun, moon,
and other constellations; beneath, in the deep cavities,
the pagans placed their Tartaros and Elysian fields.
This world, in which the universe was enclosed, was
meted out into a series of domains belonging to the
societies of respective deities. Each domain with its
natural riches is granted to a people charged by their
deity to make use of it, and to defend and extend its
power. The deities lend their assistance in this task;
they protect their people against their common enemies;
they lend their help in the defence of the State and
city; and put their people in possession of the State and
city of other gods; they favour their career and watch
over their well-being. Yet they do not offer these
services for nothing in return. From the first
they exact an entire obedience, complete submission
to all orders, and, above all, the payment as tribute
of a share of the harvest and the increase of the
cattle. Still further, whenever the people intercede
for a particular service, their prayer is not listened
to unless it be presented with humility and accom-

panied by an offering or a sacrifice. When the people disobey their commandments, when they neglect to pay their tribute, the gods punish them by letting loose tempests, plagues, and other scourges ; on the other hand, they recompense the exactitude and the zeal with which the people . acquit themselves of their duties and fulfil their obligations. In a word, the gods conduct themselves with regard to their people as an owner does in regard to his servants—the *coloni* or *métayers* to whom he has entrusted the management of a property. Here, then, is the divine act of exploitation, and the human institution upon which it is based.

The appropriation of the necessities of life appears among men as well as among the inferior species as an instance of the natural instinct of preservation. When men unite in herds, in clans, or tribes, and live by the chase and the natural fruits of the soil, each tribe claims for itself the exclusive possession and enjoyment of the lands, abundant in animal and vegetable nutrition, · which it has discovered, together with the adjoining spots on which it has established its homes in huts or caverns. The tribe prevents strangers from entering and using the territory where it had found its sustenance, and when either the population increased, or the forest game grew scarce, it is compelled to encroach upon the frontiers of neighbouring tribes. The character of this primitive appropriation was communal, or to speak more precisely, collective. The search and hunt of game did not coincide with the apportionment to individuals of the hunting grounds of .the tribe. But this apportionment and individualisation became necessary when agriculture succeeded to the chase as the staple food industry. While the hunters procured their food with less trouble and in greater abundance by combining to hunt the game throughout the whole extent of the tribal territory, which they could only with difficulty have parcelled out and enclosed, than by partitioning it out and each separately making use of his share, this was not the case with the agriculturalists. It was necessary that the agriculturalist should possess an estate belonging solely to himself, and whose produce he alone should be able to reap, otherwise he would not have given himself the trouble of clearing, ploughing, and sowing it. The domain of the tribe thus split up and individualised itself. In the countries where the soil did not require the application of capital in the form of manure or improvements, individual property was of only temporary duration ; the tribe, making use of its corporate right, reserved to itself the power of reforming the distribution of shares, by adapting the shares proportionately as the families to whom they were assigned increased or decreased in numbers. Elsewhere, in the countries where stability of tenure was necessitated by the nature of the soil and the exigencies of cultivation, individual property became perpetual. But the rapid advance in the productivity of the food industry under this new form of appropriation came to develop, if not to give birth to a series of industrial phenomena—the accumulation of capital, exchange, price, and to create fresh relations between the co-operators of production. The extent of agricultural estates soon became unequal, and the methods of cultivation and production diversified. Sometimes the estate was cultivated by the proprietor himself with his own stock and dependents, composed of his family and servants; sometimes, usually after a conquest, cultivation was abandoned to an overseer with slaves; sometimes to subjected settlers, to whom the proprietor conceded the soil and furnished in whole or in part the working stock, at the same time, laying on them the burden of partaking with him the products of the undertaking or of paying a rent.

By carrying ourselves back to these facts which have so profoundly affected the conditions of human existence, we account for this salient feature of the religious idea of the second age—the appropriation to the gods of the terrestrial domain created by them, and the concession by them of this domain to a people subjected to them as the slave, *colonus*, or *métayer* is to his master, and who in the same way yield in exchange a rent or tribute.

II. *The division of labour or the specialisation of the attributes and functions of the deities.*—In this new economic state, labour was divided and specialised. While in the primitive tribe the inadequacy of industrial productivity obliges the generality of the tribe's members to surrender themselves to the search for subsistence, in the second stage, when the food production does not absorb more than a part of the forces of the community, the industries and professions multiply, and in multiplying, become specialised

REESE LIBRARY
OF THE
UNIVERSITY
OF
CALIFORNIA.

some are cultivators, some artisans, who undertake a
great variety of businesses, some merchants, and, in
a superior class, some are warriors, and some are
priests. This development of the economic organism
typed itself in the religious idea. The divine work
divides itself as the human work is divided: the
deities multiply and specialise themselves in company
with the industries of mankind. Such a division of
labour is particularly characteristic of Paganism.
Among the numerous deities of Olympos, some are
charged with putting into force the machinery of
nature, either by directing the course of the sun or
by governing the tides of the sea ; others, in the same
way, by practising an industry, patronised by a profession or function. The rank which they were assigned
in the heavenly hierarchy corresponds with the importance attributed in the mind of the time to that
industry, profession or function.

III. *The constitution of a divine government.*—In
a tribe of hunters the government is extremely
simple. The elders formed a sort of tribal council,
and, in case of war, they chose a chief charged with
the direction of offensive or defensive operations.
But a State, in which population and wealth are advanced, and in which the multitude is subjected to a relatively smaller ruling class, demands an organisation
more complex, more stable and more strong. The association of the landowners elect a chief charged with the
care of the common security, and most often it makes
this office hereditary, in order to avoid the danger of
rivalries and internal struggles. This chief, in his

turn, chooses the staff of military and civil functionaries, whose co-operation is necessary in order that he
may acquit himself of the task assigned to him, and
each member of this staff, in his turn, nominates
his subordinates. By reason of the necessities to which
the State must minister, a hierarchy is therefore constituted. Yet harmony does not always reside in such
a government; the authority of the chief is often dis-
owned; certain discontented and ambitious ministers
conspire or openly revolt, or attempt to depose the chief
in order to put themselves in his place. This political
organisation of the States of the second age, and the
circumstances to which it gave birth are carried into
the divine government. The divine functionaries of
Paganism and the demi-gods who assist them, are
subjected to the authority of the master of Olympos,
Jupiter, the sovereign of the gods. Jupiter had to
repress the revolt of the Titans; he vanquished and
cast them down into Tartaros.

The appropriation of a State and people to its
gods, the division of labour, economic and political,
amongst the gods, which the preservation and working of this world necessitates, the constitution of a
heavenly government and hierarchy, such are the
characteristic features of the religions of the second
age. As in the case of the deities of the primitive tribes, the gods of the States who succeed
them are, for the most part, made after man's image;
they have his virtues and vices, his passions and also
his caprice, and, above all, they are, like him, obedient
to the motive-power of interest. It is *their* interest
which guides them in their relations with man. It is

their *interest* which impels them to succour, protect, injure, reward, or punish him.

Such was the religious conception of humanity in the second age ; it was that of a divine government modelled on the human government of the State or city, with gods who are only distinguished from men by the superiority of their power. Was it possible for the multitude to conceive of these gods otherwise ? Even supposing that the descendants of the magician had been able to image and offer for their adoration, deities fashioned upon another model, with other appetites, other passions, other motives than the multitude's, would they have recognised, and would they have been disposed to obey them ?

CHAPTER III.

A SOCIETY cannot exist unless it imposes a rule, or
a "law" on its members. This law consists in the
obligation to abstain from actions hurtful to the
community, and to perform those profitable to its
preservation and progress. Observations and experiences compel these hurtful or profitable actions to
be recognised. Suppose, for instance, that the
strongest or cunningest snatched away the returns
of the labour of the weakest giving nothing in
exchange, or leaving an insufficient supply of
sustenance, the weakest would perish; then the
despoilers would struggle among themselves, and,
in turn, succumb to a like fate. It is, then,
necessary for the preservation of society, that
each should, in some degree, respect the property
and liberty of another. This necessity implies,
in the first place, the recognition within their natural
limits of the individual's property and liberty with
such restrictions, liabilities (*servitudes*), as the
general and higher interest of the community en-
joins, and, secondly, the establishment of a re-
pressive and penal system which guarantees rights

21

by inflicting on those who infringe them pains in
excess of the pleasure procured by the infraction.
But this is not all. The preservation of society
necessitates not only the recognition and guarantee of
rights, but the fulfilment of a series of duties as well.
It is necessary that the members of the community
should mutually aid one another, the stronger assisting
the weaker, and that all should unite in the presence
of a common danger. This necessity is the more
urgent as the community is more exposed to dangers
from without. It is also necessary for its existence, that each generation should beget another to take
its place and should impose on itself, in consequence,
the sacrifices which the performance of this obligation
demands ; that the children should be cherished,
educated, and protected until they are of age to provide
their own living and protection ; that, on the children's side, they should assist their parents when old
age and infirmities have rendered them incapable of
supplying their own maintenance. To these obligations enjoined by the general interest of the preservation of society—to which that of the individual is
bound—are added many others. When disease, due
to uncleanliness, the consumption of putrid food, etc., is
incurred by members of the community, it is necessary
to impose on them the regular observation of clean
and sanitary habits, as well as temporary or permanent abstention from unhealthy food. Observation
and experience compel these manifold necessities to
be recognised by the more intelligent members of the
embryonic society of the first age, the clans, septs, or
tribes. But it is necessary to manipulate the masses

and oblige them to impose on themselves sacrifices, and to undergo the privations they involve.

In the absence of the intelligence and moral force which the comprehension and observance of political, moral, economic, and sanitary rules or laws exact, the religious sentiment intervened. Religion became the originator and instrument of the law. It became this by a logical process of the mind ; for did it not rest with man by making offerings and obeying the divine commands to win for himself the favour or disarm the malevolence of those higher powers who cause him his sensations of pleasure or of pain—the powers whom he conceives to be animated by instincts and passions like his own, and obedient, like himself, to self-interest? These the magician, or soothsayer, had embodied in the idols ; he is in communion with them, and he naturally attributes to them the inspiration, the "revelation" of the laws. These laws are not invariably useful, for the soothsayer is not infallible. He is more especially prone to error since the ulterior consequences of human actions are frequently at variance with their immediate results, and since an action which causes a present evil in order to effect a future good, or *vice versa*, may well appear harmful. It is also possible that the soothsayer to whom the spirits embodied in the idols reveal the law, attributes to them commandments more to his own interest than that of the people at large ; that, for instance, the spirits reserve for him and the chiefs certain choice articles in the public provision. But it was necessary that the laws should not be too manifestly in opposition to the opinion the majority has formed of the common interest, otherwise the authority of the magician would incur the risk of being compromised, and a rival more skilled in interpreting the thoughts of other minds would not be slow in supplanting him. When agreement exists, and the law is accepted, it becomes unalterable, and is quite as much observed as the religious faith : the faith in the existence of spirits and the belief in their sacred power becomes more profound and general. Each person takes care that the law is obeyed, and in case of necessity denounces those who infringe it, since every act of disobedience to the law is an injury to the spirit whose edict it is, and this injury will expose the whole tribe to inevitable chastisement.

When the breeding of live stock, the discovery of edible herbs, the invention of implements of agriculture and the first arts, the establishment under the form of slavery of security of life and products of labour, had determined the transformation of the sept, herd, tribe or clan, (the conditions of whose food industry prevented them from multiplying beyond some hundreds of beings,) into a State whose population is able to increase a hundredfold and more—then the institutions, in consequence of this progress, continued to modify themselves and the laws to multiply ; the territory of the community from which the chase had furnished food, divided itself out into portions adapted to agricultural industry, and this partitioning of the soil brought about, in consequence, the rise of the patriarchal community. The proprietor of each portion became head of a family, and continued to nourish

and govern the folk on his estate, women, children,
servants or slaves. The employments to which the
increase of elementary industry gave birth became
constituted in the same way under the form of individual enterprise, and the necessities of common protection effected their unions in associations. Exchange and price, which with difficulty existed in
the primitive herd, in which each man provided for
himself against a scanty number of wants of the
first necessity, now grew into frequent use, and
demanded the recognition of a series of rights, and the
fulfilment of a series of conventional obligations.
The agglomeration and contact of a multitude of individuals round the centres of industry and commerce,
by rendering diseases more frequent and more fright-
ful, necessitated the establishment and rigorous observation of rules relative to the cleanliness of body,
raiment, dwellings, as well as the purity of the food
supply. It was necessary to discover all these rules
indispensable to the preservation of the State and its
population, and to ensure their observation.

In the tribe of the first age, it was the magician
who, at once priest and *savant*, inspired by the tribal
spirits, formulated these rules. In the societies of the
second age, the functions of the magician, having become more numerous and complicated, passed down
to his descendants, for they alone possessed the
capacities and knowledge necessary for the task.

The descendants of the magician, either in the case of
a subjugated tribe or a dominant people, constituted,
therefore, a religious, political, learned caste, which,
thanks to its intellectual and moral superiority and

the necessity of its services, shared the government of
the State with the warrior caste. Moreover, when the
State came to be conquered by fresh barbarians, this
section of the former governing class soon recovered
its position and influence. For the barbarians were
not slow to recognise that they would not be able to
do without them in the enjoyment and preservation
of the domain they had possessed themselves of. In
the same way that the conquering army organised
itself usually under the form of a society, having as
its object the exclusive enjoyment of the conquered
State, in the same way that the classes devoted to the
material labours of production constituted themselves
into companies of agriculturists or traders, the
descendants of the magician formed a corporation or
immense caste devoted to the exercise of the diverse
professions we nowadays qualify as liberal. There
was, however, an essential difference in the practice
of these professions, as they were pursued at the
beginning of the second age and as they are nowadays; this lies in the fact that the stock of acquired
knowledge being then so inconsiderable, the professions which are now separated were then able to be,
and, in fact, were, commonly combined. After entirely satisfying the religious wants of their patrons,
the descendants of the magician continued, like their
ancestor, to practice other learned professions. The
priest was, at one and the same time, a doctor, an
astronomer, a magistrate, and a judge.

Here we have a natural association, ignorant of
scientific observation and religious intuition. What
the priest discovered or invented in the domain of

the moral, political, physical, or natural sciences, he attributed to a supernatural or divine communication, and he was still more inclined this way as his inventions and discoveries thereby secured an authority which they would not have had had they been simply of human origin. There was not, as one would have said, any deception. For, as far as that goes, had the same person still continued to provide for the religious services, to devote himself to the culture of the sciences, and the practice of the political, moral, economic, and other arts, there is no doubt that the discoveries which have enriched the sciences and the inventions which have perfected the arts would have been attributed by their authors to an inspiration, a divine revelation, in the same way as were those which have transformed the religions.

The spirits of the tribe, in their new rank of deities of the state or the city, were increased in numbers, and hierarchated, and constituted a divine government. But, this government possessing the State, and the people, taking from this property a revenue, under the form of offerings and sacrifices, had an interest not to allow the State to perish. What, therefore, should these deities do ? They revealed, in the same way as the spirits of the tribe had of old, the rules and practices necessary for the preservation of the state or people. Each time the want of a political, moral, economic, or sanitary rule made itself felt, they communicated it to the descendants of the sorcerer, who, on their side, through the increase of occasion for their services, had also increased in numbers.

In order, however, that a rule may be obeyed, a
sanction is indispensable. That sanction, which had
already appeared in the embryonic religion of the
primitive tribe, now developed and perfected itself.
It consisted in a scale of punishments, proportioned
to the gravity of harmful actions, and a scale of rewards commensurate with the utility of others. The
good, those who observe the laws and practice laid
down by the deities, are admitted to the Elysian fields
of Paganism ; the evil, those who are disobedient to
the divine commandments, are hurled down into
Tartaros. Amongst the people whose religious ideas
have not yet aspired to the immortality of the soul, the
pains inflicted and the rewards conferred by the gods
possess a purely earthly character, and, as the
masses are able to affirm that they do not always
suffer from the infraction of the law, they are the less
efficacious. The introduction of the dogma of the
immortality of the soul in the religion of the second age
has, therefore, in a great degree brought with it the
social efficacy of the divine code.

The religious faith, the belief in the existence of
superior powers or deities—possessing the State and
interested in its preservation—who show themselves so
much the more alert to procure for their people every
sort of good, and to preserve them from every sort of
evil, as they pay their dues with greater exactitude,
and obey more punctually their commandments—this
religious faith, we affirm, came therefore as the first
and indispensable mode of ensuring the preservation
and progress of human societies. The laws which
defined and assigned the limits to the rights and

duties of individuals, which interdicted harmful
practices and enjoined profitable ones — these the
deities revealed, and cause to be observed, by rewarding those who conform and punishing those
who infringe. The more religious the people, the
better the laws are observed, the less is the need
to resort to temporal power to make them respect.
At an epoch when the vast majority of men were
without either the enlightenment or the moral force
necessary for that subordination without which society
is unable to subsist, a subordination which the temporal
power was clearly incapable of establishing or maintaining, this the religious faiths at this epoch established
and maintained with a marvellous efficacy at the minimum of expense. From this fact the conclusion may be
drawn, that had the human species been destitute of
religious feeling it would have never passed beyond
the level of the other animal species. It is religion,
rather than the aptitude to invent tools, that has
created civilisation.

The religions of the first ages offer in their divine
personnel, in the attributes and manners of this *personnel*, in the laws they have revealed and the
practices they have commanded, certain more or less
marked differences. The study of comparative religion, however, shows us resemblances more numerous
and important than these differences. This is due,
on the one hand, to the fact that the human beings
who conceived the deities, and fashioned them in
their own image, resembled rather than differed from
each other; and, on the other hand, to the fact that
their associations, their societies, are not able to exist

save on the condition of submitting themselves to analogous rules of recognising and exercising like rights and duties, rights of property and liberty, duties of mutual assistance and custody. These rules are adapted to the conditions of existence in the societies, and to their degree of development. The tribal religious codes of the first age vary from those of the second; but between them there is a striking analogy. The majority of moral prescriptions in the religions of India and China—in Paganism, Christianity, and Mahommedanism—are identical, since they minister to identical needs. Variations are determined by the temperament of the peoples, the relative proportion of the sexes, climate, etc. Only, when a progressive or retrograde society, or, better still, when religion adapted to this society is imposed on peoples living under other climates, and belonging to other varieties of the human race, the religious prescriptions of morality and hygiene do not always modify themselves in adaptation to these changes; these prescrip· tions then lose a portion of their utility, and sometimes become even harmful into the bargain.

CHAPTER IV.

IN the petty societies of the first age the system of worship is not very elaborate. The magician fashions the idol in which the tribal guardian spirit embodies itself, and the amulets and charms to which the touch of the idol communicates a preservative virtue. The faithful place their idol in a dwelling-place sheltered from the weather, and sometimes clothe and ornament it with beads; they provide for its wants by offerings of food and drink; prostrating themselves before it, they offer their homage and prayers.

In the societies of the second age, the tribute paid to the deities increases with the riches of their folk, and adapts itself to the material and moral wants attributed them in accordance with their ranks and functions. Ceremonial develops itself; the rules or rites of this ceremonial become numerous and complicated. To the worship of the deities are now applied those formulas of etiquette which experience has proved to be essential to a respectful obedience of a slave to his master, of a subject to his king. The idols enshrining the deities are assimilated to their respective characters, functions, and attributes. They

31

are fashioned out of precious metals; they are robed
in rare stuffs; they are pavilioned as befits them, in
buildings surpassing in grandeur and richness the
habitations of their subjects. The servants of these
deities dress themselves in liveries or distinctive uni-
forms just as the servants of earthly kings and
grandees. The mob throng the portals of the temple
(the interior being commonly reserved for the deities
and their servants) in order to present their offerings
and address their prayers to the idol in which the
god resided. The offerings are suited to the nature
and appetite of the gods, some of whom are, like
cannibals, greedy for flesh and blood, and only to be
appeased by the sacrifice of human beings or eatable
animals—beef, mutton, venison; while others of a
softer disposition prefer milk, honey, fruit, or incense.
The priests receive these offerings, immolate the victims,
present the milk, honey and fruits, and burn the
incense on the altar. Forms expressive of humility
are invented for purposes of prayer and adoration,
rites are instituted for offerings and sacrifices, and, in
short, for all the relations of man with the gods.
Like men themselves, the gods have a taste for the
fine arts, and are particularly sensible to music.
Feasts of music are therefore provided, dread and
mournful cords are struck when supplication is made
to the gods who preside over the works of destruction
and death, while the music in the Temple of Venus
is soft and voluptuous. By a reflex action these
strains excite in the bosoms of the adorers sentiments
and passions which they attribute to the objects of
their adoration. The rites of worship becoming fixed

pass through a period of elaboration. Whenever a part of the ceremonial—vestments, attitudes, instrumental or vocal music—is not in harmony with the character the devotees attribute to their deity, the discord strikes them as a false note, and they naturally imagine that the unpleasing sensation produced upon them is shared also by the deity himself. The cultus is thus rendered perfect by this unconscious collaboration of the faithful in proportion as the cultus satisfies the religious concept. The rites and the ceremonial at least tend to become fixed and immutable.

The religious systems of different peoples, however, only approximate in varying degrees to the religious ideal they have in view. The divine concept which constitutes their spiritual element varies in elevation and purity with the amount of intelligence, morality, religious capacity possessed by those who conceived the deities existence and their disciples. The material element which is comprised by the idols, images, temples and ceremonies depends upon the current artistic talent, taste and riches of each people.

Except in the case of the tribes too poor to support a magician, every cultus has its minister. But how is provision made for the maintenance of this staff of servants of the gods, for the creation and supply of the material of religion ? In the States which had undergone conquest—and this was almost universally the case in the second age of humanity—the warrior conquerors of the State were, for purposes of government and administration, compelled to have recourse to the enlightenment and knowledge of the descendants of the magician, and repay their assistance by aban-·

c

doning to them a portion of the conquered domain,
together with its stock of human creatures. These
donations of property, the descendants of the magician,
now become the sacerdotal caste, turned to good purpose, and drew from thence a revenue which it employed on the construction, furnishing and preservation
of the temples, and construction and adornment of the
idols abiding there. To this revenue accruing from
its inalienable possessions, were added chance sums
accruing from the offerings of gifts in kind and of
money. Cattle, and formerly—when in default of
cattle man was the prey of man—human victims,
milk, fruits, grapes and other eatables were offered to
the gods; a portion of these gifts was abandoned to
their ministers, in the same way that the dessert on
the masters' tables was left for the servants. The
amount of these offerings was proportioned to the
depth and extent of the religious sentiment, and of
the riches of the people, and also in respect to the
popularity the deities enjoyed, and the particular efficacy attributed to each idol. Every time a demand
is made upon a god for advice upon the opportune-
ness of an expedition or anything else, a payment
must be made in consideration for the service. The
revenue of the religious domains, together with these
casual sums, constitutes a sufficiency which procures
an independent existence for the majority of the religious of the second age.

CHAPTER V.

THROUGHOUT the first age, and at the beginning of the second, the essential character of the religions is their mutual exclusiveness. Each tribe, and later, each nation, has its own peculiar gods, whose jurisdiction does not range beyond the frontiers of their territory. This exclusiveness sprang from two causes—(1) the identification of human and divine government; (2) the original isolation in which the tribes, and later, the nations, composing humanity were wont to dwell.

In their character of proprietors, the gods governed their State; they dictated the rules of conduct, defined the obligations of their subjects, and sanctioned them by menacing transgressors with chastisements; they protected their people against their enemies, and indeed, partook in its contests, procuring victory when victory was merited by rigorous observance of their laws, assiduity in worship, and unceasing supplies of offerings; on the other hand, they ceased to protect it—save when not to do so would involve their own dispossession—and rendered no assistance in battle when their laws were forgotten or neglected. That is why war was never engaged in, or a battle commenced,

35

REESE LIBRARY
OF THE
UNIVERSITY
OF
CALIFORNIA.

without their first being consulted. At the moment of commencing warfare, sacrifices were offered up and their aid besought. After a victory thanks were rendered and a recompense made from the spoil of the conquered. After a defeat, attempts were made to regain their favour by observing their laws more closely than before, by punishing with twofold severity those who infringed them, and by increasing the number of sacrifices.

This divine government, however, was only able to enunciate its orders by employing the services of intermediaries, to whom it delegated the powers of putting them into execution. These intermediaries and delegates constituted the human government of the State. In their capacity as ministers of the deities they governed the State, or chose the chief or king charged with the government. From such persons the chief elected by the delegates obtained his authority. Here, then, we find the origin of the "divine right of kings." The laws which the chief of the governing hierarchy is charged to put into action are the laws of religion. For this very reason we are unable to conceive how more religions than one could exist side by side in the same State. Was it, in fact, possible to alter the cultus, to adore new gods without at the same time inflicting a blow on the claims of the old ones ? for in that case would not tribute cease to be paid ? Would the gods and the agents, who, in transmitting to them this tribute, became entitled to a share, contentedly put up with this loss and resign themselves to the consequent diminution of their revenue ? Would they also allow a portion of their subjects to cease observing their laws and to place themselves not merely under alien but even adverse deities? The case would be aggravated when the national religion was abandoned for that of a strange and, therefore, of a hostile people. To do this was to place in the hands of inimical gods the tribute due to one's own natural deities, and to place oneself at the disposal of the hostile deities and their emissaries, who were compassing the downfall of the fatherland. It was, in short, as if a Frenchman refused to pay taxes to his own Government in order to furnish funds for the German, and, in event of war, enlisted in the German service. To forsake one's own gods for foreign ones was to become a traitor to one's country. This is why it was held necessary to inflict on renegades the penalties of treason. The deities were without mercy in this respect; the God of the Jews authorised the massacre of the misbelieving Israelites who had deserted His altars for those of Baal.

Furthermore, in the original state of isolation in which each tribe or nation carried on its earliest existence, they only had cognisance of their own respective gods, and remained in complete ignorance of those of the other tribes or nations. Yet even when the latter became known to them, they would hardly have been disposed to adore the gods who acted as guardians of tribes with whom they stood on hostile relations. In order to induce a people to reject its gods and choose others, it was necessary to drive them to extremities either by excessive demands of tributes and offerings, or else by the severity of their laws. Such an emergency must, doubtless, have

occurred, but if the revolt were repressed the old
deities retained their sway; if, on the other hand, the
new were victorious the new took their place. In either
case, religious unity remained intact, and the divine
government continued to be identified with the
human.

Progress of different kinds has, however, in the
course of time effected the separation of these two
governments, or, as we should nowadays say, of
Church and State. As a consequence of this the
co-existence in the same State of more religions than
one has also been rendered possible.

In the later centuries which preceded the appearance of Christianity, religion no longer possessed in
the civilised world about the Mediterranean, which
alone 'demands present - attention, the preponderating influence it had enjoyed at its first start. The
arts and sciences had so developed that their further
progress entailed an extension of the division of
labour. At first, the descendants of the magician, at
one and the same time priests, legislators, magistrates,
doctors, artists, etc., compelled to acquire a more considerable body of knowledge and to minister to the
requirements of an increasing *clientèle*, divided
among themselves the occupations which they had
originally combined together. Amongst these occupations were some not only foreign to religion
but even of a nature calculated to diminish faith in
its dogmas; such was medicine, which discovers other
causes of disease than the ill-will or anger of the gods,
and other remedies than amulets; such, again, was
astronomy, which by the observation of astral move-

ments suggested hypotheses out of harmony with belief in the deities entrusted with the guidance of these movements ; such, again, was philosophy, which brought these explanations to a fair degree of advance, and constructed out of them a synthesis. Little by little, therefore, science separated itself from religion, even if it did not become actually opposed to it. A separation similar, although infinitely more important in its result, effected itself between the functions of the cult and those of the State. In societies where the productive power had increased and population and material wealth been augmented, the legislative, administrative, and judicial functions came to be separated in the same manner as the arts and sciences. There came into several existence in these places magistrates, judges, and administrators. Little by little from the accumulation of their resolutions and decisions there was evolved a political, civil, and economic code distinct from and more complete than the religious code. Religion still continued to hold sway over all the conduct of life ; it sanctioned the decisions of the magistrate and the verdicts of the judge ; but, in fact, the human government had emerged from beneath the divine. The State had become a lay thing. It was henceforth possible to remain the subject of the State, even when one had ceased to belong to the established religion.

To these factors of progress, which caused in prac-tice a separation of Church and State yet to be worked out in theory, must be added the progress of industry and commerce, which had established pacific relations among the various folks. Limited in its origin

to the frontiers of each separate State by lack of security
and means of communication, commerce had, by creep-
ing along the courses of rivers and coasts of seas,
gradually extended itself. It ran along the borders
of the Mediterranean, and threw out branches
even to the Indian Ocean and the Atlantic. The
Phœnicians founded the source of their fortune in
the exchange of the products of the East with those
of the West. The Greeks—and notably the Athenians
—sprung from a Phœnician colony,[1] followed their
suit. Of the articles of exchange, the most important.
was man himself ; the slave trade excelled all others
in extent and value, and caused the bringing
together and intermixing of persons belonging to
different religions and nationalities. Under the influence of the Roman peace and the effectual repression of piracy, the commerce of the Mediterranean
basin acquired a more and more considerable development. The Jews, at this point, undertook an
increasing share in all this, either as usurers or as
merchants. After the destruction of Jerusalem, they
were compelled to spread in masses throughout Asia
Minor, Greece, and even Rome.

In this new state of things, in which the barriers
hitherto appertaining to human or divine governments were relaxed; in which commerce had established relations of mutual interest in the midst of
the peoples comprised by the Roman rule, and
created markets at which persons belonging to every
kind of religion met as buyers or sellers, the religions,
developed by the combination of all these points

[1] [This is a theory.]

of progress, ventured beyond the frontiers to which
they had hitherto been confined, and their disciples came to meet each other elsewhere than on
fields of battle; and it was at this moment, that a
new religion appeared, destined, in due time, to
supersede all ancient ones and become the religion of
our civilised world.

This religion made its appearance at an opportune
moment. Some centuries later, when the bonds
which fastened religion to the State were again
intact, and when incessant warfare had wiped out the
lines of commerce, its propagation would have been
impossible. And, further, at the actual moment of
its appearance, the exclusive cults of Paganism were
in full decadence, and now but imperfectly answered
the needs they aimed at supplying.

Religious monopoly had, in the long run, effected
all the results common to every sort of monopoly ; it
had engendered mere routine, negligence, and extravagance. In possession of wealth accumulated during
ages of domination, devoid of the stimulus of competition, the pagan priest devoted himself too little to
the masses too poor to furnish the gods with a really
valuable tribute, and willingly consigned his attention
to patrons of the middle and higher classes. But in
these classes, the educated minority, who had been to
the school of the philosophers, and, consequently, lost
their faith in the old gods, followed the practices of
the established religion with only just sufficient
zeal to escape the penalties of the law and
the reprobation of the faithful. The majority held
on by tradition and custom rather than by conviction.

Moreover, some of the pagan deities authorised and enjoined actions which the progress of civilisation and wealth condemned as immoral and harmful. If the cult of Mercury, patron of robbers, did no injury to the received ideas of an age when piracy was held in honour, and when a robber was, as at Sparta, considered a man of parts, this certainly ceased to be the case in a commercial age, when movable property was considerably respected, and the development of commercial relationships had accentuated the harmful character of the raids made by the worshippers of the messenger of the gods. The feasts of Venus and the Bacchanalian revels, by their coarse and immoral exhibitions, in no less degree, gave offence to manners, more decent and refined, if not actually better. However, the indulgence of the pagan priest could be obtained when infractions of morality were redeemed by the richness of the offering.

Such, then, was the state of Paganism, when certain schismatic Jews, persecuted by the priesthood and the faithful of the State religion, spread themselves, as the Imperial peace allowed them to do, throughout the countries under Roman rule. The new religion they brought with them possessed a morality incontestably superior to the old religions, and, moreover, possessed a character and advantages which was bound to render it peculiarly winning to the masses.

CHAPTER VI.

Natura nihil facit per saltum. This can be said
with equal truth of the human mind. In order that
a man may receive a new idea in religion, morals, or
science, it is necessary that this idea should not differ
entirely from the one to which he has previously been
accustomed, that he should find points of agreement
between the old idea and the new, and be able to
make these serve as bridges by which he may pass
from the one to the other. We have seen what constituted the religious idea at the epoch when the
States of the second age succeeded to the primitive
tribe. This idea was that of a heavenly government
modelled upon the earthly. This government was
proprietor of the State's soil and population; it was
constituted, as every government is, by a people under
a hierarchy, and the authority of a supreme lord. To
this last the subject people had to pay a tribute, and
make their obeisance under the pain of exposing themselves to punishments proportioned to the gravity of the
delinquencies and the duties of subjection. Such was
the common basis of all religious ideas, and this basis
which we have found in Paganism, we shall find again
with but slight differences in form, and singular points
43

of analogy, in Judaism, the mother religion [1] of Christianity.

According to the book of Genesis, God brought the world out of chaos; He created man and granted him the enjoyment of the fairest portion of this universe on condition of his being obedient to His commandments, and not evading the duties of a faithful subject. The explanation of this condition is afforded by an analogy of the revolt of the Titans against Jupiter. Like all the chiefs of the State, the God of the Jews possesses His hierarchy of officers or functionaries, angels, archangels, seraphims. This hierarchy exercised the functions and filled the offices which devolved on the hierarchical governments in the patriarchal states or despotisms, such as existed in the second age of civilisation, and such as still may be found in Asia; it formed the court of the sovereign, executed his orders and assisted in the administration of his domains. But even in the less closely constituted and ordered states, it produced conspiracies and revolts against the sovereign. One of the great officers of the heavenly hierarchy, giving way to the temptations of a perverse ambition and unbounded pride, rebelled against Jehovah, and attempted to drive Him out. Jehovah conquered and pitched him and his accomplices into the outer darkness. But, being either unable or undesirous of persuing him, He permitted him to establish himself there and

---

[1] [The Translator, following English custom, has used capitals in expressing the names and attributes of the One True God. He hopes, that he has in any degree, not, thereby, deprived M. de Molinari's work of its scientific character.]

found a kingdom. When Jehovah created man, what did the rebel angel Satan do? This aristocratic creature was covetous, and attempted to divert and obtain for himself the obedience man owed his Creator. He succeeded in this by incarnating himself in the most cunning of beasts, the serpent. Jehovah punished man for his disobedience—the greatest and least excusable of crimes in the eyes of an absolute sovereign—by driving him out of Eden, and condemning him to live by the work of his hands—a penalty which must have seemed particularly severe at a time when the inadequacy and imperfection of tillage rendered tillage at once most painful and least profitable. However, the sons of men continued to obey the suggestions of the rebel angel. To destroy this ungrateful race, therefore, Jehovah had recourse to the deluge. A single man, a single family, found grace in His sight. Once more He singled out in the descendants of this family, a people—the Jews —whom He protected and governed to the exclusion of the rest of the human race. But, even amongst the chosen people, the original sin of disobedience checked the attainment of any great result. This crime of divine high treason, as all other crimes, could not be otherwise redeemed than by expiatory sacrifice; but such is the dignity of the offended, and such is the weakness of the offenders, that the latter are unable to offer a sacrifice of sufficient merit to recompense the offence. This compensation can only be afforded by a being of equal rank with Him who has been offended, a divine being, a Messiah. The Jewish people awaited, then, the

advent of a Messiah, who was to sacrifice Himself in
order to wipe out the original transgression, to re-
concile the creature with his Creator, and replace him
in the state of salvation in which he was before the
fall. This Messiah, this Saviour, predicted by the
prophets, appeared in due time in Judea. But the
majority of the Jewish people refused to recognise
Him. The Priests and Pharisees compelled them to
put Him to death as an impostor. The Jews con-
tinue to exist as if the Messiah had never come ; re-
fusing the new law of Christ, they preserve intact the
old law of Moses, and will preserve it until the appearance of the true Messiah. This is the dogmatic
idea of Judaism.

It was from this conception, differing as it did in
form rather than in essence from other religions, and
in full accordance with the moral and judicial ideas of
the times, that Christianity was born. While the
majority of the Jewish people, obedient to its priests
and submissive to the influence of the conservative
Pharisees, refused to recognise the Messiah in a carpenter's son, a minority, composed of humble men,
recognised Him by His miraculous power, and accepted His law. In the eyes of this minority, soon to
be swelled by the enrolment of Gentiles, the Christ is
the Son of God, He is of one substance with Him, He
is one of the elements of the Divine Trinity—power,
love, intelligence,—He is the true Messiah. By this
title He possesses the power to offer satisfaction for
the wrong offered the majesty of the Sovereign of
Heaven and of earth, and is able to redeem the original
sin by offering Himself as a sacrifice.

This conception of redemption by a sacrifice equivalent to the offence and the injury caused by it, was a product of observation and experience in penal jurisprudence, and is to be found in the majority of ancient systems of law. Among the Teutonic folks it gave rise to the establishment of a *wer gild* (*i.e.*, redemption —money proportioned to the gravity of the offence). In the same way the consubstantial trinity of the Divine Personality (*la consubstantialité trinitaire de la personalité divine*), which is also to be found in the primitive religions of India, was a product of human introspection. In considering his distinctive nature, man recognised in his normal being power, love, and intelligence, and he was bound to transfer this trinity of his being to the Deity who had fashioned him in His own image. The Divine Being, doubtless, differed from his own in degree. Man, therefore, represented the Deity as an infinite power, an infinite love, an infinite intelligence. Would he otherwise have been able to conceive of elements of which he had no notion? The Trinity of the Divine Essence was, then, as it could not but be, a human trinity infinitely expanded. The Father represented power ; the Son, compassion or love ; the Holy Ghost, intelligence.[1]

[1] [The Translator feels bound to make some brief comments on the above paragraph. He ventures to think that M. de Molinari has inadequately conceived the teaching of the Church on this point. "The Catholic faith is : That we worship one God in Trinity, and Trinity in Unity : neither confounding the Persons : nor dividing in substance." However useful the nature of man might be in the *explanation* of this dogma, as mere matter of history, the dogma preceded the explanation, and not the ex-

These two conceptions, redemption by sacrifice and the adaptation of the human to the divine nature, the former familiar to minds even the least developed, the latter easily accessible, logically coincided with all the other dogmas of the new faith.   Could that one of the Three Divine Persons, who by His nature must be drawn to sacrifice Himself for the redemption of the original sin of humanity, be other than He who was the expression of compassion or love ?   And how could He be able to accomplish this sacrifice in any other way than by becoming incarnate, and offering that which is most precious in man—His blood, His life ?

Christ, however, only ransomed those who promised for themselves and their children to obey His law.   These received baptism, which washed away the original sin of disobedience.   But to be received into the heavenly kingdom, baptism did not suffice.   It was necessary that the baptised Christian should, during his earthly life, be obedient to the divine law, and this law, like that of Judaism and the other religions, extended itself to all the manifestations of human activity.   It defined the duties of each individual towards God, towards the Church, to which Christ had delegated His spiritual power, towards his neighbour, etc. etc.   These duties are specified in a twofold

planation the dogma.   To say, as some have said, that the Son represented compassion and love, as the Father represented an angry and omnipotent Deity, is to forget that in Christ's teaching God so loved the world, that He gave His only begotten Son to the end, etc., St. John iii. 16.   The whole matter of the *explanation* afforded by human introspection is well dealt with by the Abbé Gratry in his *Connaisiance de L'Ame*, vol. 1.]

code, religious and moral, pronounced or revealed by God Himself in the person of His Son, interpreted, developed, applied by His earthly administration,— His Church, whose chief, inspired by Him, is infallible, as He is Himself, and as are all the powers existing at this period.

To summarise, the God of Christianity answers to the ideal which had been at that time fashioned of the head of a State. He loves His people to such a degree as to be interested in the welfare of even the most humble individuals; He is a Master, watchful, good, just and pitiful, but at the same time He is an absolute master, who desires that His law shall be obeyed. Like every sovereign at this epoch, He does not recognise any rights in His subjects. The most exemplary observation of His code does not confer the right to be admitted into His Heavenly Kingdom. It constitutes simply a plea for admission. It is the Sovereign, the Lord, who is the judge of the worth of the plea. According to His pleasure He admits or rejects the postulant.· It is a grace He accords, not a right He recognises. For the rest, such is man's imperfection that he is not able to act in such a manner as to merit His grace without divine assistance, and this assistance, which procures for Him the moral force necessary to conquer his besetting sins and to keep the law of the Lord, is granted or withheld at the Lord's good pleasure. Only, since He is just and good in the highest degree, in that He is all that a ruler of a State ought to be, He does not withhold these gifts from those whom He thinks have by their works or effusion of faith and love sufficiently applied them-

REESE LIBRARY
OF THE
UNIVERSITY
OF
CALIFORNIA

selves to merit it. But the number is small ; many
are called and few are chosen. For man is still
affected by the fall of his first parents. He is prone to
evil, and is also assailed by the temptations of the
devil, who watches for opportunities of peopling
his domains. It is a constant struggle between the
good and evil tendencies—between his desire to obey
the law and his inclination to infringe it, and such is
his infirmity and such is the rigour of the law, that
he rarely chances to be the conqueror in this strife,
and falls therefore under the sway of the penalties
that guard the sanctity of the law. Doubtless God is
not only just, He is merciful as well, but His mercy
has its limits fixed by justice itself. A sovereign
cannot tolerate the infringement of his laws without
losing his authority, or allowing his good things to
pass into the hands of evil doers. If then, God rewards
some, He punishes others. The reward consists in
admission into the heavenly realm, and the contem-
plation of the Sovereign's face, a thing which in the
ideas of the times was the most exalted favour that
could be offered a subject. This reward was to be
obtained immediately when all the duties presented
in the divine code were fulfilled, or only after a period
of proof and penitence—purgatory. The punishments
consisted in the definite refusal of admission to the
heavenly kingdom, and eternal relegation to the lower
regions where the damned are prey to the rebel
powers, the devils who are confined there, who,
obedient to their malignant nature, are busied
in torturing their victims. Such sentences are
taken from the stock of earthly justice, and chosen

as the most cruel. In this again divine justice answers to the ideas of the time. Disobedience to the divine law implies an offence to the majesty of the most puissant and august of sovereigns—the King of kings; the punishment ought to be suited less to the gravity of offence than to the quality of him who is offended. Such in general outline is the conception of Christianity.

The advantages which Christianity possessed over Paganism were of two kinds—moral and material: both resulting from the difference in the conception of the divine motive. The motive which the gods of Paganism pursued was their own proper interest; and they governed their people with a view to exacting tribute, and only rendered their services on the prior condition of being repaid. The motive of the God of the Christians is, on the contrary, the love of men, and their interest, not His own. He did not exact anything more for Himself than the return of His love and obedience to laws made with a view to man's well-being. He did not exact the payment of any tribute, and it was not necessary to strengthen by costly offerings intercessions offered him for any favours or service. The pagan Olympos was filled with a host of deities, each having his particular function and jurisdiction, to whom it was necessary to make a present for each service coming under their respective offices. In the room of these swarming greedy deities, whose services were reserved for the rich capable of paying them, Christianity had but one God, and this God was all-powerful, able to grant all sorts of favours and render all sorts of services, asking in exchange neither sacrifice nor offering. But more, He accorded these favours, He rendered these services to the poor as well as to the rich. His ministers—His apostles—contented themselves with what was necessary, and, for the most part, lived by the work of their hands. The most illustrious of them, St. Paul, said if a man will not work neither shall he eat, and he preached by example, seeking his living by tent-making. In a word, Paganism was an expensive religion, Christianity a cheap one.

CHAPTER VII.

IN opposition to Paganism, Christianity possessed an indisputable economic and moral superiority, yet a religion, like an industry, can only aggrandise itself or supplant its rivals by entering into active competition with them. Thus, at the epoch of the identification of religion and the State, when each separate people had its own peculiar gods, the mutual relations of the varying gods and peoples being of an exclusively hostile nature, there could not possibly have been any sort of religious propaganda. As the gods had entered into the warfare of their peoples, the conquerors, after having gained possession of the lands of the conquered, whom they enslaved if they did not massacre, did not fail to proscribe the hostile deities, to destroy their images and burn their temples. The dispossessed would, if allowed to place themselves under the protection of the triumphant deities, abandon the gods who had already abandoned them. Each people were, nevertheless, zealous of their gods, and that not without reason. They would not suffer their ancient foes, now become their slaves, to share in their religion, and to obtain thereby favours and protection which might be turned against themselves. They pro-

53

hibited, therefore, access to their temples, and this prohibition applied also to the strangers, whom the development of trade, effected by the advance in industry and navigation, brought to commercial towns like Athens. This state of things continued even when it had been found more convenient to substitute for the massacre or the enslaving of the conquered people a simple tribute, and to allow them, as the Romans did in Judea, their institutions, laws, and worship. The refusal to allow foreigners to participate in the national worship was completed by the refusal of liberty to join a foreign religion. For, if the State deities were deprived of the increase in their revenue, which would have been brought them by an increase in the number of their devotees, was it not but equitable that the alien deities should be prevented from further diminishing their revenue by claiming a share of the tribute rendered them by their own nation ? To refuse them the compensation of protection against foreign competition would be to provoke their just wrath. The result of this twofold prohibition was to render all religious propaganda impossible.

It seemed, then, that Christianity would be destined to remain confined to the narrow region of Judea, where it was born. If it had been so confined, it might well be asked whether it could possibly have emerged from the active persecution to which it was put by the Jewish priesthood, whose monopoly it threatened. This persecution, however, preserved it, and brought about its expansion. Prosecuted and hunted down in Judea, the makers and propagators of the schism in the established religion emigrated, for the most part, into neighbouring lands. Like all proselytes, they were anxious to spread their faith. The propaganda, moreover, contributed to supply the means of existence which the poor refugees could only find with difficulty. In theory this propaganda was forbidden in Asia Minor and in the other countries whither the Christians fled, but the pagan priesthood were less easily aroused, and believed themselves less interested than the Jews in putting the law into action. As long as the Christians remained few in numbers, and won over their adherents from the poorer and lower classes, and so did no material injury to the established religion, the pagan priesthood did not bestir themselves, and were content to ignore their obscure opponents.

It was otherwise, however, when the new religion by the quality and number of its converts had acquired a serious importance. Then, but too late, Paganism invoked the assistance of the State in order to preserve their monopoly, just as the priests of Judaism had done at the advent of the Christian Messiah. This appeal to the civil arm was so far justifiable in that the Christians, in the zeal of their faith, showed themselves less tolerant than the pagans. They did not confine their energies to pacific, oral or literary methods of propaganda, but actually destroyed the temples and upset the images of the gods of Paganism. An aggressive religion, not to be satisfied with the toleration meted out to its fellows, conniving at the expulsion of the tutelary deities of the Empire and the enthronement of its God in their room, clearly came under the rigour of the laws protecting the

State religion. These laws and the penalties attaching to them were then considered quite as necessary as we now consider the regulations in modern codes which protect the industries possessing a monopoly, or monopolised by the State itself. This explains why even the most just and humane of the Cæsars, such for instance as the Antonies, did not scruple to place the law in full action.

Yet this condition of protection did not suffice to save Paganism; it may indeed have hastened its downfall.[1] The moment arrived when, after three centuries of struggle, Christianity clearly surpassed its rival in numbers and in power. Then the pagan Cæsar, in order to escape the imminent risk of being dispossessed by some Christian Cæsar, turned himself to the victorious faith. In embracing Christianity, Constantine carefully abstained from placing Paganism, still influential, under the ban, and consequently, for close upon two centuries, the struggle continued with varying fortunes. During the reaction, patronised if not provoked by the Emperor Julian, it seemed as if Paganism would win back its supremacy, but this was merely a forlorn hope. Christianity had acquired a decisive predominancy. In conformity to the character of the times, it employed its advantage for the destruction of its rival, and in so doing, availed itself of

---

[1] [M. Gaston Boissier has shown how reliance upon the State was one of the paramount causes of the downfall of Paganism, and that the Christians were cognisant of their advantage in this respect.] Cf. *La Fin du Paganisme*, vol. ii., pp. 269, 330. Later, when Paganism had been conquered, the Christians having changed their mind, Christianity became a State religion, and from being persecuted, it became the persecutor

the weapons that had been used against itself—confiscation and punishment. Let us notice that when the time of the Protestant Reformation arrived, this spoliation of the pagan priesthood served as a precedent for the imperial spoliation of the old faith in the interest of the new.

By the fifth century of our era, we may consider the struggle as over. Christianity had replaced Paganism. The temples of the latter had been demolished or transformed into churches, the property of the old religion confiscated to the State, the favourites of the court, or the new religion ; yet this revolution had been less profound than we are accustomed to suppose. The religious *clientèle* were the same, and it was necessary that the services they demanded should be adapted to their intellectual and moral condition. The most numerous portion of the population, the slaves, serfs, or peasants, by the very nature of their occupations, enjoyed but a feeble intellectual development. Excluded, in the past, from the State religion, they only experienced such religious needs as could ordinarily be satisfied by the adoration of fetiches, and the wearing of cheaply procured amulets, to which they believed that the touch of idols had communicated the virtue of preserving the wearer from all kinds of evils and diseases. Above the ignorant and superstitious masses was a half-cultivated class of persons who, even when philosophers' doubt had destroyed the faith of the upper classes, still remained faithful to the old gods. In closing the pagan Olympos and in throwing open its churches to even the poorest devotees, Christianity

purified religion, while it at the same time extended
its area. Yet this culture had to be brought to the
doors of the worshippers of idols as well as to those
of the adorers of fetiches. Christianity was, therefore, compelled to accommodate itself to the pagan
conception of a celestial government with its hier·
archy of gods and demi-gods respectively devoted to
the numerous and diverse functions necessitated by
the protection of a people and the satisfaction of their
material and moral needs. It was not long before
this government reconstituted itself in the minds of
the Christian masses, but under different forms and
denominations, although with similar attributes. God
the Father, God the Son, the Holy Ghost, the Virgin
Mother, the archangels and angels, and the legion of
saints, incessantly increased by canonisations (which
replaced the deification of heroes and emperors whom
Paganism had admitted into its pantheon), took
the place of hierarchical deities of Paganism, and
specialised themselves in a similar way. The Christian artists depicted God the Father with His Son on
His right, and beneath, in gradations, the dignitaries
of the heavenly court, according to their rank, and with
the forms and features and dress, which the popular
imagination attributed to them. In the same way
that the mass of persons solicitous of offices, favours,
and graces, are unable to address themselves directly
to the sovereign, emperor or king, who governs the
earthly State, the simple and ignorant people could
not conceive it possible that the Sovereign of the
heavenly State would himself receive every request,
and that the recommendation or intervention of an

influential person at His Court would be valueless. The substitution of one religion for another was unable to free the popular mind of a conception founded upon the observation and experience of human affairs. Instead, therefore, of addressing themselves to the gods and demi-gods, the people besought the intervention of the Virgin, the angels, and saints. In short, Christianity paganised itself in order that it might reach the masses still merged in Paganism. Among the higher and more educated classes, to whom the schools of philosophy had already suggested the central idea of monotheism, the dogmas of Christianity were able to win acceptance with less concession and fewer compromises. Yet, even here, this was not the case as far as the economic side of Christian doctrine was concerned. The community of goods, conformable to the teaching of the Messiah, if not actually enjoined by Him, and practised by the first Christians, could not commend itself to a class of proprietors. It was necessary to abandon this point and to limit Christianity to a recommendation to the rich to succour the poor.[1]

In like manner, Christianity was compelled to accommodate itself to the political necessities of the times. The first Christians had not sought for possession of the State. Had not Christ Himself said, "My Kingdom is not of this world?" We have, however,

---

[1] Gaston Boissier : *La Fin du Paganisme*, vol. ii., p. 402. [We ought to notice that it was to a professing Christian St. Peter said :—" While it remained was it not thine own ? and after it was sold, was it not in thy power ?" (Acts v. 4). *Cf.* W. T. Simcox : *Early Church History*, ch. i.]

seen that in the societies of antiquity, religious law covered the whole civil and political life, and that two or more religions with their respective laws, could not co-exist within the same State, without the risk of anarchy. Religious unity and the union of religion with the State were indispensable to interior order as well as external safety. In this respect, matters gradually became modified. The laws of the Roman Empire, while preserving this ancient religious formalism, were codified by jurists, and put into action by magistrates who did not exercise sacerdotal functions. The separation of Church and State, together with a plurality of religions, had become possible, and that without any risk to external safety or internal order. The experiment had, indeed, been made under Constantine and certain of his successors, but a new fact is always in conflict with old ideas, and long centuries were destined to roll by before the human mind, still imbued with the necessity of religious unity, even when that unity no longer existed, was able to conceive the possibility of the separation of religion from the State, and of the possibility of toleration.

CHAPTER VIII.

So far from retarding the progress of Christianity, the invasion of the barbarians hastened its advance. It raised the clergy to a higher position than they had held under the rule of Rome. The tribes of Goths, Franks, Vandals, and Suevi who invaded the Empire, and ended by establishing themselves there, found themselves under the necessity of constituting a vaster and more complicated government than that which had suited a tribe. For it did not suffice merely to share in the conquered territories; it was necessary to turn them to profit. Ignorant, and, to a great extent, without ideas of administration, or even of arithmetic, the peoples were compelled, in order to manage their domains and keep their accounts, to call in the assistance of the class in possession of the necessary knowledge which they lacked. The Christian clergy occupied an elevated rank in the lettered classes, and possessed over the barbarians a superiority analogous to that nowadays possessed by our missionaries over the backward peoples of Africa and the Pacific. At the same time, the pomp of worship, and the glamour of its ceremonies, exercised over the minds of these new-

comers into civilisation an impression of wonder and
respect. While the class of State functionaries and
scribes remained tacitly hostile to these brutal and
uncultured barbarians, the Christian clergy, animated
by the spirit of proselytism, set to work to conciliate
them with a view to eradicating their idolatry as well
as preserving their own goods and position. The
barbarians, moreover, ignorant as they were, well
understood the influence the clergy possessed over
the subjected people, and recognised the importance of
their co-operation in the task of keeping the masses
in order. These considerations of interest, added to the
natural ascendancy which a cultivated class exercises
over uncultivated minds, effected their speedy con-
version. By this superiority in education and knowledge, the Christian religion found its position and
prestige increased and fortified. Without express
acknowledgment, the new masters of the State, by
respecting their property, and increasing it by
donations, and the right of raising a tax called the
tithe, specially designed to provide for the necessities
of worship, and by warding off, more carefully than
the Cæsars had done, any attack on clerical monopoly, submitted to the ascendancy of the clergy, and
remunerated their assistance. At the same time, the old
cults or idolatries and schisms which menaced the privileged religion were rigorously prohibited. In all the
monarchies springing from the barbarian conquest,
Christianity became the religion of the State, and by
this title was invested with a monopoly even more
absolute than any which had existed under the Roman
Empire.

A twofold interest, material and moral, incited the Christian clergy to keep this monopoly intact. The moral interest was, indeed, the insult which would be offered to God Himself by the toleration in the same vicinity of a lying religion—a devil's agency: the material was the preservation of the Church's goods, and indeed of its very existence. For the admission of a new religion would infallibly have entailed the eviction of the old, the expulsion, and, it may well be, the massacre of the priests. Again, if idolatry and paganism ceased to afford cause for fear, it was not so with the schisms. It was no unusual occurrence for the conquering Christians to become divided among themselves, and for antagonistic parties to spring up in their midst. Whenever one of these dissenting parties or schisms chanced to get the best, it took the place of defeated orthodoxy, and did not fail to possess itself of the spoils of the orthodox clergy. This affords an explanation of the extraordinary violence of religious quarrels; the object of the conquest being, not merely the realisation of a programme, often but slightly differing from that of the party in possession of the State-conferred monopoly, but indeed to win that position for themselves.

Despite these struggles, which more often than otherwise had the effect of reviving religion, the early centuries following the fall of the Empire form the most flourishing time of Christianity. Recruited from the pick of the people, the Christian clergy exercised a preponderating influence in the government of new states, preserved the legacy of antiquity, and, thanks to the peculiar security they enjoyed, effected within the enclosures of their monasteries the revival of agriculture. They were the promoters of every great enterprise, and, by appealing to religious feeling, the spirit of adventure and the desire for gain, for close on three centuries, drew vast herds of men off to the crusades.

Unfortunately, to this period of constitutional security, in which the increase of population had been encouraged to the highest degree by the development of feudalism, a period of material decadence succeeded. The disruption of feudalism and the increase of anarchy put an end to the extraordinary prosperity which the Christian world had enjoyed from the eleventh to the thirteenth centuries. When bad days had come and with them penury of resources, the spiritual and temporal powers, which up till now had remained united, commenced at last to quarrel. The struggle began about a question of money (the investitures struggle), and this dispute soon spread itself throughout all the countries of Christendom. It is easily seen why the spiritual power had from the first the superiority in this struggle. Thanks to the donations made by the kings and the masses of the faithful, and the revenue afforded by her landed property and casual gifts, the Church had become the greatest proprietor and financial power in all the states where she existed. She was mistress of education, and presided over all the acts of life, birth, marriage, death ; she held souls by the fear of punishments, and the hope of rewards beyond the tomb. Her chief, the sovereign pontiff, in his character of representative of God upon earth, constrained the most powerful

and refractory of monarchs by a simple menace
of excommunication, that is to say, of religious
outlawry. All the states of Christendom paid him
tribute.

However, two different causes—the degradation of
religious work and the moral corruption engendered
by monopoly—were at work to destroy this enormous
power, and to secure the progressive secularisation of
government and law.

In the first ages of the barbarian monarchies, the
clergy had given voice to the law, and furnished the
greater portion of the governing body. But at
Rome as in the past, outside the pale of religion, little
by little, there was formed a class of legists and
administrators. While clerical celibacy rendered it
impossible for the priests to render their offices
hereditary, these lay legists and administrators both
increased in number and perpetuated their class by
hereditary transmission of office, the children usually
following the profession of their parents. It was upon
these rivals of the clergy that the kings relied in
their struggles with the latter, and, thanks to their
aid, they disembarrassed themselves of their guardian-
ship.

In the same period, the monopoly possessed by the
Church—a monopoly which from the fifth to the
sixteenth century no schism was able to break through,
worked out its usual results—slackness and corruption. The immense riches which the Church had accumulated during this long space of time rendered her
more and more independent of those who otherwise
would have insisted on her services. The clergy con-

E

stituted the most powerful of corporations, and such was the conduct and customs of its members that no one could meddle with it without exposing himself to the dangerous charge of heresy. It would not suffer any external control. However rigid may be the watch a political, industrial or religious body places upon itself at its commencement, this control will soon slacken; the more important members of the body, those whose superior position places them above control, are the first to exceed the limits the rules place upon them, and their example can hardly fail to be followed in the lower ranks. The manners of the secular and regular clergy, from age to age, grew worse and worse, and they showed less and less zeal in the fulfilment of their religious duties. The increasing corruption of their morals diminished the authority they had enjoyed, and gave birth to a reprobation which expressed itself in satires and caricatures, until at last the spirit of criticism engendered the spirit of revolt. The services which this enervated and protected clergy supplied were depreciated in value without any diminution in price. In the palmy days of the Middle Ages, such prices did not seem excessive, but now that bad times had come, the people, who had been ruined by anarchy and war, found themselves hard pushed to pay the sums they once had considered light. Religious buildings commenced in times of prosperity now remained unfinished, and since everything fetched a smaller price, the tithe and other ecclesiastical sources of income became gradually more and more onerous. Amongst the people, religious feeling grew dim and inactive, whilst the display of clerical villainy provoked men of superior minds to violent reaction. This reaction gave birth to the Reformation.

CHAPTER IX.

THE REFORMATION AND THE RELIGIOUS WARS — THE PHILOSOPHIC REACTION OF THE EIGHTEENTH CENTURY.

SLACKNESS and corruption had in time sapped the material force of the Roman Church, and caused a deficit in its finances. The ordinary revenues of the clergy did not suffice to cover the proud and luxurious extravagance of her high dignitaries and to provide for the expenses of the sumptuous edifices they still continued to erect. The ecclesiastical government issued therefore a sort of paper money which, according to their own account, would secure currency in the heavenly kingdom as payment for the redemption of sins. A rich man would, by fortifying himself with the right amount of this paper money, be able to gain admission to the dwelling of the blessed, and this even after a free career of vice, avarice, luxuriousness, and covetousness. One had nothing to do but pay over the price. In Southern countries, as in Spain and Italy, where morals declined under the influence of climate, the issue of indulgences met with favour and found an excellent market; but it was otherwise in the Northern lands, where already the depravity of the clergy had produced grave scandal. The sale of indulgences was, so to speak, the "last drop of water which makes the vessel overflow." Religious souls were indignant at this sale of sacred things, and demanded the reform of the abuses that had crept into the Church. Instead of listening to this protest, the ecclesiastical government met it by excommunicating the "Protestants." The reformers then transformed themselves into revolutionists. Preserving the essential dogmas of Christianity, they tore away from religion its outward cloak of pomp and luxury; they abolished the discredited monastic orders whose riches excited the covetous-minded; to the dictatorial rule of the Roman Church they opposed the parliamentary government of an elective assembly. In Germany, and in the other countries of the North, public opinion pronounced itself in general accord with the reform party, and the sovereigns gave in their adhesion. Apart from the religious feeling which influenced some of their number, they were induced to take this course both from a fear of the results of a conflict with dominant opinion, and by the opportunities of profit which the confiscation of the property of the monasteries and clergy offered them. It cannot be forgotten that in England, at least, this last consideration exercised a decisive influence on the mind of Henry VIII. On the other hand, in the countries where Protestantism only enlisted in its cause a minority of the upper and middle classes—in Italy, Spain, France, and the Southern Netherlands—the sovereign remained loyal to the Roman Church.

In all these countries, the Church was united to the

REESE LIBRARY
OF THE
UNIVERSITY
OF
CALIFORNIA

State, and no one as yet dreamed of their separation. The Reformation, however, by giving birth to a struggle for existence, could but bring about the destruction of religious monopoly. The governments which had adopted Protestantism interdicted the practice of Catholic worship, possessed themselves of the property of the clergy, demolished the Church, or attached them to the new religion. In the countries remaining Catholic, Protestantism, *à fortiori*, was absolutely proscribed. The Inquisition was called into being in order to track down and hand the makers and adepts of schism over to the secular arm. On both sides alike, on the side of the new religion as well as of the old, recourse was made to torture and the stake in order that the religion of the State might be protected from rivalry. In Italy and in Spain, where the cold and severe ceremonial of Protestantism was antipathetic to the artistic character and instincts of the people, and where a strain of Paganism was innate in the masses, there was little or no struggle at all. But in France, where Protestantism had gained a considerable portion of the rich and cultivated class, things were different. Here the Reformation gave rise to the civil war, which Henry IV. ended by a compromise in the " Edict of Nantes." This compromise, Louis XIV., a sovereign actuated by the old idea of the necessary coincidence of Church and State, committed the enormous fault of revoking, much to the detriment of the moral power and material prosperity of the kingdom. In the Northern Netherlands, the heresy, which had conquered the majority of the population, remained

victorious, while it was extirpated throughout the
Southern Netherlands, where, as in France, it had
only gained a minority respectable in quality, but
insufficient in numbers. It was only when one of
these religions, the new or the old, had secured its
monopoly that the wars known as the wars of religion
were brought to a termination.

The rival cults, however, did not obtain a State monopoly gratuitously. After having imposed their conditions upon the State, in the epoch when the barbarous
monarchs stood in need of their assistance for the organisation or security of their rule, the clergy, whenever the
secular arm was needed to defend their monopoly in
Catholic countries, or to obtain it for them in the Protestant—the clergy, we say, were compelled to accept conditions which it was now the State's to impose. Now,
however, the Church had more need of the State than
the State had need of the Church; and the latter power,
therefore, came to be ruled as of old she had been the
ruler. Louis XIV. for instance, while restoring
the monopoly of Catholicism, subjected it to the
régime created by the declaration of 1682 (which
restricted the power of the Pope by asserting the
power of State), and also made no scruple about laying
hands on the property of the clergy.

In England, the head of the State in like manner
imposed his supremacy on the Established Church,
and, into the bargain, he compelled her to put up
with the rivalry of dissident schisms which formed
themselves into independent bodies. In short, the
Church—Catholic or Protestant—was wholly or par-
tially protected against competition; but this pro-

tection was purchased at the price of her independence and liberty. It could only procure for her a deceptive security and prepare the way for her downfall.

The harmful influence which is inherent in any monopoly affecting human activities did not fail, therefore, to make itself felt in religious culture. The sloth and corruption which had provoked the Reformation, and had been effectually remedied in the sixteenth century by competition, again made their appearance and increased with rapidity in the eighteenth. In Catholic countries, the clergy, still in possession of vast domains and protected against all competition, showed themselves less active and zealous in the fulfilment of their duties. In Protestant countries, where the property of the clergy had for the most been confiscated, and where in the place of the Catholic religion, which was generally prohibited, the established religion was compelled to cope with the dissenting sects, religious culture, if not actually progressive, yet preserved more or less of its purity. Not having a rich patrimony at their disposal, the Protestant clergy found themselves obliged to appeal to the good-will of their patrons for a great portion of their means of existence, and it was therefore their interest to stimulate devotion. The inferior Catholic clergy were enslaved to the power of the dignitaries, and, being then reduced to a position similar to that of the Protestant pastors, and possessing but a comparative independence, they expended in the exercise of their offices an activity as great as their assurance of reward was slight.

To this recrudescence of faith, which the struggles of religion had stirred up, there succeeded in turn luke-warmness, indifference, and soon even hostility. Perhaps also the violence of persecution, the odious proceedings of the Inquisition, the crimes committed in the pretended interests of the faith, had contributed their share to a reaction against a religion, whose interests had so often enjoined acts in complete discordance with the prescriptions of Gospel morality.[1] A philosophic school formed itself in correspondence with this new tendency of thought, and served as the expression of nascent reaction.

Up till now, the philosophers, the enemies, and critics of the gods, who, in the name of reason, attacked dogmas without offering in their place any fresh ones or a new faith, had found but a feeble echo in the cultured classes. But by the revocation of the "Edict of Nantes" they acquired at a blow an extraordinary amount of favour. With the re-establishment of religious uniformity, and the end of religious controversy in France, there also came into active existence a literature not simply schismatic but frankly anti-religious, deistic, indeed even atheistic. It attempted to demolish dogmas, to qualify revelation as an act of imposture, and to show it up by bringing to light what one might call the wrong side of religion— the wrong-doing of every sort it has caused, the crimes it has inspired or sanctioned. This so-called philo-

[1] [Mr. John Morley, in his *Diderot and the Encyclopædists*, speaks of the French Church of the eighteenth century as evincing a "strange mixture of Byzantine decrepitude and the fury of the Holy Office."]

sophic literature, together with the memory still
fresh in men's minds of persecutions and the culpable
sloth of a clergy grovelling in riches, awakened in the
cultivated of the Christian World a sympathy with
those lines in *Tragedy of Mahomet* :—

> " The priesthood is a vain contrivance.
> Our credulity is its single science."

In other times, when the assistance of the Church
had been indispensable to the State, this aggressive
literature, which employed without mercy the in-
vincible arms of irony and satire, which ridiculed
even the most venerable of traditions, which did not
dissemble its intention of attacking the faith it styled
superstition or fanaticism, would have been rigorously
repressed, and its authors would have expiated their
diabolical blasphemies at the stake.   But now the
situation was altered.   The State was no longer dependent on the Church.   It possessed a political,
judicial, and administrative staff, recruited almost entirely from without her ranks.   It was emancipated from
her tutelage, and the time had come when her past services could be forgotten.   Perhaps, also, the material
loss caused by the revocation of the "Edict of Nantes"
had stirred up in the mind of the governing classes an
unconscious resentment against a society whose protection was so costly.   If, however, the State had
succeeded in restricting the communications of the
great clerical corporation with its foreign chief, this
corporation none the less possessed immense riches
and power, and also enjoyed, from a fiscal point of

view, exceptional privileges. It was freed from the obligation of some of the most profitable taxes, and, with the assistance of the State, gathered its own peculiar tax, the tithe. This explains why the State dealt gently with an institution with which it was, however, now able to dispense, and it also shows us why, in the growing financial embarrassment, the State threw covetous glances towards the riches which the Church had accumulated under its protection, and which offered an inadequate contribution to its imposts.[1]

If no outbreak had arisen, this reaction stirred up by religious monopoly would probably have resulted in the repeal of the prohibition against Dissent,[2] and the subjection of clerical property to the law of fiscal equality. It may also be conjectured that the Catholic Church, like her rivals, would, in course of time, have been compelled to content herself with the voluntary offerings of the faithful, and that this step would have been followed by a more equitable redistribution of incomes among the superior and lower clergy. But the Revolution broke forth, and with it the State fell into the hands of politicians, who, imbued with the anti-religious doctrines of the eighteenth century, were growing daily more and more hostile to the clergy. Moreover, these parvenus of the Revolution had, like all other parvenus, an insatiable

---

[1] [The place of the Church in the fiscal system—if it can be called a system — of the *Ancien Régime* is well described in Lowell's *France before the Revolution*.]

[2] As early as 1787 the practice of the Protestant religion ceased to be contraband.

appetite for rule or authority. The State they personified was incapable of tolerating within its pale any power capable of resisting its sovereign will. This is why the revolutionists did not limit themselves to suppressing the privileges of the corporations, but suppressed all corporations, including even commercial and academic associations. Having imposed upon the clergy and the monastic orders a "constitution," they confiscated its property, and reduced the ministers of religion to the condition of State-appointed, State-paid, and State-ruled functionaries. To the legitimate protests of the clergy, they replied by the prohibition of Catholic worship, and they sought to replace it—the deists by the worship of the Supreme Being, the atheists by the worship of Reason. Since, however, these novel religions did not succeed in making proselytes, it became necessary to tolerate the old. Religious needs, deprived during the play of revolutionary persecution of their means of satisfaction, demanded, with an appetite provoked by so long a fast, the food it had been accustomed to. The churches were re-opened, worship was reconstituted, and everything sanctioned the idea that the Church would soon find sufficient resources in the contributions of the faithful. Nevertheless the day of religious liberty was not yet come. France had to fall under the yoke of a despot, who rendered the Church the favours of the State, but compelled her to pay as her price the larger part of her independence and liberty.[1]

[1] The following extract from the Catechism of the Empire will show at what a cost the Church has purchased its enrolment on the budget :—

Catechism for use in all the Churches of the French Empire.

Edn. 1806. Part II. Moral. Lesson VII. Continuation of
Fourth Commandment.

Q. What are the duties of Christians to ruling princes, and in
particular to Napoleon I., our Emperor?

A. Christians owe to ruling princes, and in particular we owe
to Napoleon I., our Emperor, love, respect, obedience, military
service, the tributes ordained for the preservation and defence
of the Empire and his throne ; we also owe him fervent prayers
for his safety, and for the spiritual and temporal prosperity of the
State.

Q. Why are we bound to all these duties towards our
Emperor?

A. Firstly, because God, who creates emperors and directs
them according to His will, in crowning our Emperor with
gifts, has made him the minister of His power and His image
upon earth. To honour and serve our Emperor is to honour
and serve God Himself. Secondly, because our Saviour Jesus
Christ has, by His teaching as by His example, Himself taught
us what we owe to our Sovereign. He was born on the occasion
of a submission to the edict of Augustus Cæsar ; He paid the
prescribed tax, and in the same way that He has enjoined the
duty to render to God the things that are God's, He has also
enjoined that of rendering to Cæsar the things that are Cæsar's.

Q. But are there not some special motives which ought to
attach us more especially to Napoleon I., our Emperor?

A. Yes ; for it is he whom God has raised up under severe
straits to re-establish the public worship of the holy religion of
our fathers, and to be its protector. By his profound and active
wisdom he has restored and preserved public order ; by his
powerful arm he has defended the realm ; by the consecration
he has received at the hands of the Sovereign Pontiff, the head
of the Universal Church, he has become the Lord's anointed.

Q. What ought we to think of those who fail in their duty towards our Emperor ?

A. According to Paul, the Holy Apostle, they withstand the order established by God Himself, and render themselves deserving of eternal damnation.

Q. Do the duties by which we are bound to our Emperor bind us equally to his legitimate successors in the order established by the Constitution of the Empire ?

A. Yes, beyond doubt, for we read in Holy Scripture that God, the Lord of heaven and earth, by the council of His supreme will and providence, granted Empire, not only to one particular person, but to his family as well.

Extract from the Minutes of the Secretary of State.

PALACE OF THE TUILERIES,
April 4th, 1806.

Napoleon, Emperor of the French and King of Italy,
            On the report of our Minister of Worship, we have decreed, and do decree, that,

Art. 1. In execution of Order 39 of *the law of* 18 *Germinal, An. X.,* the Catechism annexed to the present decree, approved by His Eminence the Cardinal Legate, shall be published, and alone be in use in all the Catholic churches of France.

Art. 2. Our Minister of Worship will watch the printing of this Catechism, and, during the lapse of ten years, he is especially authorised to observe such precautions as he may think necessary.

Art. 3. The present decree will be printed at the head of each copy of the Catechism, and inserted in the *Bulletin des Lois.*

Art. 4. Our Minister of Religion is charged with the execution of the present decree.

(Signed)   NAPOLEON.

By the Emperor,

The Secretary of State (Signed)   HUGUES B. MARET.

Certified.

The Minister of Religion (Signed)   PORTALIS.

See also the form of oath imposed on the bishops by the *Concordat.*   [*Cf.* Jervis.   *Church of France,* vol. ii., ch. xi.]

CHAPTER X.

AT the commencement of this work we have said that the state most favourable to the development of religious liberty and the improvement of religious culture is that in which Church and State are separated, and we notice that this opinion is beginning to spread among the intelligent *élite* of the clergy. Yet in admitting this fact, is it well to wish that this state of things should be established, and that liberty should procure for religion a renewal of vitality and influence? In plain terms, are religions beneficial or the reverse? What has been their influence in the past of humanity? Has this influence been for good or for evil? Have they favoured or opposed the progress of the human mind, furthered or thrown impediments in the way of the march of civilisation? Is it, in consequence, desirable that they should be suffered to perpetuate themselves or, on the contrary, should be allowed to disappear? And, if it should be demonstrated that they are nought else than social evils, would it not be better to inhibit them, or at the very least, so far from allowing them full scope, to limit them narrowly?

It will, then, be necessary to prepare an estimate of

religions, to sum up and value on the one side
the services they have rendered societies and individuals (which constitutes their *positive* side), and
on the other the expense they have cost .and the
evils of which they have been the source (which
constitutes their *negative* side).

Before everything else we ought to reckon on the *positive* side of religion the discovery, the putting into action
and the observation of laws and (more generally) of
moral practices without which no human association
would have been able to carry on its existence.
Beyond all doubt it is primarily not a religious but an
economic motive of pleasure and profit which compels
men to organise themselves. Primarily it is to protect themselves against animals better provided with
natural powers, and secondarily to profit by the increase
in pleasure and the economy of toil resulting from the
co-operation of forces and the division of labour that
men gathered themselves together and formed septs,
clans, tribes, and later, nations. But no society is
able to subsist save on two conditions:—(1) that
the associates subordinate their peculiar and epheme-
ral interests to the general and permanent interests
of the association; (2) that they also abstain from
mutual injury and devote themselves to mutual
co-operation. These conditions necessary to the preservation and progress of society, the divine government, which had its origin in the nascent religious
ideas of early ages, compels men to recognise and
observe, and this with the greatest possible efficacy
and the minimum of expense.

According to these ideas, reduced to their simplest

F

form, the spirits or gods were the proprietors of the domain occupied by their folk whom they protected, watching over their well-being, the inflicting upon them regular tribute, and subjecting them to the rules of conduct communicated to them through the agency of their ministers, the magicians or prophets. By carefully conforming themselves to these rules, the folk obtained the favour of the deities, and their goods were rendered susceptible of increase; by infringing them they would, on the other hand, expose themselves to their anger and the chastisements it was in their power to inflict. Amidst the peoples sufficiently advanced to conceive of the immortality of the soul, this system of pains and penalties when extended to life of infinite duration, acquired naturally a still further degree of efficacy.

These laws and practices which the gods imparted to their magicians or prophets were, in truth, always more or less imperfect and defective, but, if we bear in mind that they were conceived by those who were, under the existing circumstances, the most capable, we shall recognise that they were beyond all measure more useful than would have been laws and practices asserted by the suffrage of a mob not far advanced beyond bestiality. Was not this faith in a being from whose sway nobody, however powerful, was able to withdraw himself, an instrument of order of incomparable power? At an epoch when all the forces which nascent society had at its disposal were necessary for the assurance of safety from without, in default of religion, it would have been necessary, in order to maintain internal order, to have recourse to a system of terror, a system certainly incapable of checking its own abuses. Without religious belief, the maintenance of order, even if we admit, as we hardly can, its possibility, would have been everywhere most costly and uncertain.

To this primary service which religion rendered society in the early ages, we must add its no less precious services to individuals. If man is not abandoned to himself, if there exist all-powerful beings who interest themselves in his lot, is he not able, in even the most trying circumstances, in adversity the most profound, to hope for succour from on high and a restoration of his happiness? If he has been the victim of some injustice, if he has suffered persecution, is he not able to find consolation in the thought that his persecutors will not escape from the divine judgment? Among the peoples who not even possess the idea of the immortality of the soul, belief in the tutelary intervention of the gods is an abundant source of hope and consolation. With this belief, the evils of the present life, cruel as they are—physical misfortunes, maladies, and infirmities, moral pains, the reverse of fortune—become supportable, and the inequality of condition and riches no longer excited envy and covetousness in the breasts of the poor. For is not this inequality but transient, and will it not be amply compensated for in a future that knows no ending? Among the favoured of fortune, is not fear for the future a salutary bridle on the abuse of power and wealth?

Such services then even the most imperfect religions—fetichism and idolatry—have rendered society

REESE LIBRARY
OF THE
UNIVERSITY
OF
CALIFORNIA

and the individual; it follows, therefore, *à fortiori*, that these good things are to be also attributed to Christianity, which has strengthened and purified religious faith by substituting in the relationship of God to man love for interest.

Such, then, is the *positive* side of religion.

In the *negative* side, we must first enumerate the expense of worship, the price of religious work. Under the *régime* of monopoly, this price came to be exaggerated, since the practice was settled by custom ; but under the *régime* of competition it is not possible to exceed the necessary. Among other articles of the *positive*, we must mention (1) the harm resulting from persistence, not to say the immutability, of the laws, customs, and practices enjoined by religion, when, through the agency of a change in the conditions of the existence of a society, these from being originally useful have become detrimental ; (2) the evils caused by intolerance, the wars and persecutions of religion. In examining the causes of the so-called religious wars, however, it is always necessary to distinguish between political and economic motives, and those which are purely religious; (3) The evils engendered by the corruption of religious practices, the absolution for immoral acts, or, indeed, for criminal ones purchased by offerings or donations to the gods, or to speak more plainly, to their ministers.

But, to set the evil at the highest possible valuation, the *negative* side of religions is certainly not one-hundredth part of their *positive*.

CHAPTER XI.

HISTORY attests the utility of religion; yet, great as this utility may have been, religion would sooner or later have been condemned to disappear if it had not, in some degree, represented the truth, or if science, by showing its origin and examining its proofs, had demonstrated that it is based on illusions, errors, or dreams. What actually is the truth in this respect? In what, indeed, does the conflict between religion and science consist? How, in the first place, did it arise?

We have stated that at first religion and science were united, and that as long as their union subsisted, religion busied itself with the explanation of phenomena properly belonging to the province of science. The magician, who was both priest and philosopher attributed, like the masses themselves, all good or evil occurrences to spirits possessed of supernatural power. We have also stated that a separation between science and religion was in course of time effected under the influence of two causes: (1) the increase of the stock of human knowledge which, little by little, necessitated its specialisation; (2) the increase of the religious *clientèle*, which led to the augmentation of the priestly body and necessitated more and more an exclusive restriction of their attention to the offices of religion.

Although history does not enlighten us on this point, we are able to infer that at certain epochs, in countries as Egypt, India, and Chaldea, where religious functions and liberal professions and sciences remained concentrated in the priestly class, conflicts arose between the priests who had devoted themselves exclusively to the offices of religion and those who were especially dedicated to the culture of the sciences. *A fortiori*, then, this would be the case in countries where, as in Greece, the culture of the sciences and of letters became independent of religion and secular schools of philosophy came into existence.

These scientific novelties the priest was naturally prone to oppose; because, in the first place, he was unaccustomed to the methods by which they were obtained; and, secondly, because they were contrary to the science of his ancestors—the religious science of which he was the depositary. To maintain that his science, derived as it was from the gods themselves, was not infallible, was to undermine the authority of religion. If the phenomena which religion attributed to the intervention of deities operated through the action of natural causes, these deities would be but impotent idlers! What good could be effected by prayers and offerings to such beings? What could be gained by sacrifices to Jupiter to escape the fire of heaven, to Neptune to escape from tempests, if Jupiter did not hurl the thunderbolts, if Neptune was not the lord who troubles or calms the waves? Even much later, when Christianity had succeeded to

Paganism, this theory of natural law still tended to detract from the *rôle* of divine providence and diminish the importance of the saints who had in the popular imagination replaced the demi-gods. To what purpose would it be to address to the Virgin and the saints supplications for a change of weather, or the aversion of a plague, if temperature and plagues, and other physical effects are ruled by natural laws?

Modern science, by depriving the earth of its former preponderating and even unique position, and relegating it to the rank of the secondary members of the innumerable systems that constitute the universe, has brought against ancient beliefs a charge even more grave. According to the religious tradition, the sun and other celestial bodies exist only for the earth's benefit, and God Himself had no other business but man. It was to save this privileged being that the Son of God offered Himself as a sacrifice. Would not this sacrifice seem disproportionate if the earth, instead of being the sole focus of life, the only globe of intelligent beings made in their Creator's image, figures only in the lowest ranks of a multitude of worlds; if, to employ an analogy, man only found himself placed on a lower step of the ladder of being?

The seeming antagonism between science and religion is, then, explained, for it is not by any single discovery of science that religion has been discredited.[1] By wrecking the childish conceptions

---

[1] According to Mr. Draper this antagonism is indissoluble, and there can be no reconciliation between science and religion. A refutation of this theory, by the Abbé de Broglie, may be found in *Le Correspondant*, November, 1892. *Cf.* Draper, *Conflict of Religion and Science*, p. 45.

humanity formed of God and itself, by re-assigning
to man and the earth their place in the universe, by
restoring to natural law the physical phenomena
which once necessitated divine intervention and
formed the supernatural kingdom, has not science
effected the destruction of religion and finally superseded it?

We do not forget that this is an opinion fairly
generally spread in the scientific as well as in the
religious worlds. But is it well founded? May we
not, on the contrary, contend that the progress of
science in reality purifies religion, by compelling it to
replace its ancient proofs of God's existence by such
new and more decisive ones as science itself furnishes,
and thus magnifies and elevates the conception
of the divine ideal? By availing ourselves of the
gifts of science, we are able, from the very fact
of the existence of the religious instinct, to
deduce the existence of a superior power, to whom
man finds himself subordinated. This instinct
possesses a universal character. It exists and has
existed, albeit in varying degrees, from all times in
the mass of human creatures. It is distinct from all
other instincts — paternal, filial, or conjugal love,
sympathy for other men or for other species. Science
demonstrates that none of the faculties of man, none
of the physical or moral forces which constitute his
being are without their utility, that all fulfil a necessary function and answer to an object or existing
being. In the same way that the existence of the
paternal instinct proves that of the family, the existence of the religious instinct proves that of God.

If science has encroached upon some sides of the domain of the activity of the God whom religious instinct attests and suffices in itself alone to attest, has it not at the same time infinitely aggrandised it? If Apollo no longer drives the chariot of the sun, if Jupiter has ceased to hurl his thunderbolts, is this to say that, to borrow a famous phrase, "science has done with this hypothesis" (*la science puisse se passer cette hypothese*)? Is this to say that matter under the impulsion of its own internal laws acts of itself, that it produces by the mechanical operation of these laws the vital organisms of vegetable and animal species as well as the world which they serve to inhabit? Is this to say that the moral forces, intelligence, will, love, bestowed in diverse and varying qualities on man, and on the greater part, if not the whole lower species, do not exist outside terrestrial humanity and the animal world? Does not the spectacle of the universe reveal their presence and unceasing action? Of a surety, when one takes stock of the enormous capital of knowledge that humanity has accumulated, the inventions that it has multiplied for the building up of the mechanism of its civilisation, one is astounded by the magnitude of moral and intellectual energy it has expended. Yet what are our most ingenious implements, our most perfect machines, in comparison with the marvellous organisms of the animal and vegetable species? Can we admit that these organisms, so perfect, so vastly differentiated, are the products of brute forces of nature? Although as yet we know but little of the mode of the world's creation, and the preservation of order in the universe, does not the little that we do know attest the existence of an infinite and intelligent energy, stirring up movement in matter, and transforming it unceasingly? It may be, says someone, that intelligence is at work, but it is an unconscious intelligence: man alone possesses a conscious intelligence: there is in the universe no being superior to him.[1] How do we know this? And can this proud pretention be justified by an appeal to reason? Will it not suffice to merely observe the beings who people the environment in which we live, or merely observe ourselves? Are we not able to state that the intelligence is all the more conscious of its existence and actions in proportion to the power with which it displays itself? Is not consciousness possessed in higher degree by the human species, and by its chosen members than by the lower species? How is it possible to suppose that an intelligence, whose works are infinitely superior to man's, should itself be without consciousness?

It is apparent that science, if it has wrecked primitive and crude conceptions of God, has done so to replace them by a religious conception different indeed, but far more profound. We now conceive God to be a power, an intelligence, an infinite love. He is not the God of a single people and of a single world, but the God of a limitless universe.

Science, in like manner, by elevating and purifying, transforms the relations of man with God. Prayer, which in the primitive religions has most often for

[1] This theory is stated by the economist, Dupont de Nemours, M. Renan states that he and his friend Berthelot finally adopted it in the early months of 1846. *Cf. Souvenirs d'Enfance,*

its object the obtainment of certain material favours
in return for no less material offerings—prayer, which
is nothing more than a sort of bargain made with a
member of the hierarchy or divine court, becomes in
a religious state enlightened by science, a simple demand for succour, for support in the hardships of life,
and for resistance to the temptations which oppose
themselves to the fulfilment of duty, that is to say,
the end assigned to the species. For, again, it is a
truth brought to light by science that the human
species, as all others, has a necessary task to accomplish, and that humanity is endowed with the physical
and moral forces requisite for its fulfilment. These
forces, according to their good or evil use, increase or
diminish. The successive individuals who form
humanity ought, in consequence, to impose upon
themselves as a rule of life the law in the nearest conformity with the general interest of the species—the
one most calculated to secure its preservation in space
and time, so that they may, as completely as possible,
perfect the function assigned humanity in the universal
order. This profitable rule of action, observation and
experience will lay bare; but to follow it men have
need of a moral force sufficiently powerful to discipline
and restrain the appetites impelling them to infringe
it. The man who does not possess this force is able to
obtain it by asking Him who is its source . . . of such a
sort is prayer. Science, then purifies religious feelings
by ever magnifying and elevating the conception of
the existence of God.

CHAPTER XII.

As we have already remarked, the dogma of the immortality of the soul is not common to all religions. In the earliest times a belief in another life existed only in the superior races. It was believed that the dead continued to live under the sod beneath which they were buried, and that they there experienced the same wants as they had felt during their earthly life. This is why the people brought food to the tombs, sacrificed the warrior's horse to supply him with a steed, and killed slaves in order that they might serve him. At a much later date the conception of the immortality of soul freed itself, in part at least, of this gross character. The soul is now nothing more than a spirit. It passes from one body into another; indeed, it belongs sometimes to a different species from the former one. It enters the body which it animates, and, with it, will ultimately share the joys of Paradise or the pains of hell.

Without interfering with those religious concepts which do not admit of verifiable data, science contributes two sorts of presumptions, if not proofs, to the belief in the immortality of the soul. The first of these is the doctrine of the conservation of energy. In the material world nothing is lost; nothing is destroyed. Transformations occur; but there is no such thing as entire destruction. But, if matter and the forces which govern it are indestructible, if they are persistent throughout all changes, is there not foundation for believing that it is not otherwise with the moral forces? If the materials which constitute the physical being subsist, may we not presume that this is also true of the constituent elements of the moral being? Is not this at least a reasonable presumption? Yet, borrowed as it is from the physical sciences, it will not suffice to prove the maintenance of conscious personal existence. Those who cultivate the sciences have a marked tendency to consider the dissolution of one's moral being as an inevitable consequence of that of the physical. But this inadequate presumption is complemented by another, drawn from sciences of a higher order, *viz.* those sciences which demonstrate that the maintenance of conscious existence, or, in other words, that the idea of the immortality of the soul, is necessary to religion and morals. These two presumptions taken together almost amount to the nature of proof.

The religious necessity of the immortality of the soul is evident. For, if the soul dissolves itself into the great space of moral elements, as the body decomposes itself into its material elements, would not this amount to annihilation? If this is so, what matters to us the existence or non-existence of God? What have we to do with a God whom we shall never know? If, in the childhood of humanity, it was possible to

believe in the necessity of rendering worship to the
gods whose sole business was man, and to offer presents to obtain their benevolence or disarm their
malevolence, can this necessity be insisted upon at a
time when science has replaced the supernatural intervention of gods in earthly affairs by the action
of natural law? Why should man impose upon himself the cost of the worship of a Deity who does not
regard his actions, and from whom, in the short duration of man's existence, no service may be expected?
Are we brought into existence simply to leave it? If
life is sweet for some, it is bitter for others, and it
only too frequently happens that the balance of life is
weighed down by an excess of suffering. If it should
chance to be demonstrated that the existence of man
is limited to this earth, religion would lose its *raison
d'etre* for at least the intelligent few who are not content with the childish conception of the constant intervention of the Deity in the distribution of the good
things and the infliction of the evil in this world.

Morality, like religion, can only exist on the basis
of the conscious continuance of self. Man can less
easily separate himself from religion than he can from
those moral claims, whose observation is essential to
the preservation and progress of the human species.

To each of the successive individuals who constitute
the human species, morality prescribes the duty of
subordinating his interest, and in case of necessity, of
sacrificing it to that of the community. But if human
existence is limited to this earth, will not the individual
find it profitable to satisfy his interest at the expense
of that of the community, and thereby fail in the

duties prescribed by morality? It is true that in this case he exposes himself to a threefold rebuke (placing aside the penalties and recompenses of religion), *viz.* (1) that of public opinion; (2) that of social justice and power; (3) that of the conscience. But the two first are always uncertain, and the third only influences noble natures. Morality, then, has no sure basis in the hypothesis of the mortality of the soul. It has, on the other hand, a sure foundation in that of the immortality of the soul—the divine justice supplementing the insufficiency of humanity and repairing its errors. But can it be affirmed that the advance of public opinion and the apparatus of repression, joined to that of the individual conscience, will one day assure the observance of duty without it being necessary to have recourse to this double hypothesis of the immortality of the soul and a divine justice? Perhaps! But this consummation has not yet been attained, and may it not be conceived that it will never be? Opinion, restraint, conscience, are, and will by nature remain, fallible. Would conscience, apart from the intervention of religious feeling and its attendant faiths, have been able to accomplish that degree of progress which it has accomplished—the progress which leads the chosen few of the species to obey duty, apart from all considerations of restraint. opinion, and religion? How would a man, accustomed to evade duty, have been able to school himself to follow it, and to develop the germs of conscience if he had not been aroused by fear of chastisement and the hope of reward which belief in the immortality of the soul and faith in divine justice alone could stir up?

The sanction of the conscience may be able to dispense with religion, but, without the aid of the latter, it would never have been able to form and develop itself. Does not the religious doctrine of the immortality of the soul then prove itself to be the necessary basis of morality, and does not this necessity attest a fact?

Although, as will be seen, the discoveries of science are of such a nature as to strengthen religious ideas, it can not possibly be denied that, *prima facie*, they appear to militate with the facts of religion. For this reason, it would seem most probable that the antagonism which has existed during this century will not cease immediately.

The discoveries of science seem to be inconvenient for religion, since they compel it to make progress. Every progress commences by injuring the identical interests it is destined to serve, and so encounters their enmity. No new mechanical discovery in industry, no new system in science, is accepted until after a resistance, more or less keen and lengthy. The workers employed in old-fashioned industries break the machines which deprive them of the wages of employment, or altogether render their special skill useless, and force them to acquire another. Learned men and physicians combine against a system which dethrones the conceptions to which they are accustomed, and obliges some to renounce the views upon which their reputations are founded, and the rest to resort to new text-books. The machine will, however, serve the ultimate interests of the workers by elevating the quality of the retribution of their toil; the system will benefit the *savants* by enriching their science.

But these effects take time to come into play, while the injury is immediate. For this reason, we do not wonder if we find the clergy attempt to break the new machine (*e.g.*, the system of Galileo), despite the fact that this very system has elevated and ennobled the conception of divine power, and has contributed to increase in man the reverence which is one of the constituent elements in religious life. We ought not, then, to be astounded at the ill-will and bad grace with which the Catholic and Protestant clergy have assailed the recent discoveries of natural science opposed to the sacred books; these things must needs be an embarrassment and annoyance before they can be rendered profitable.

Again, the discoveries of science appear detrimental to religion, since they substitute natural explanations for the supernatural causes by which religion explains a host of facts. Science seems to trench upon the domain of the supernatural in order to extend its own. Yet the evil it inflicts on the one hand we have seen that it amply compensates on the other. Whatever may be the progress of the positive sciences, there are certain notions which will always remain beyond them, since the human mind is unable to comprehend them; such are the ideas of infinity, space, and time. These constitute the region of the unknowable, and this region, over whose borders science cannot pass each discovery proves to be more expansive and impenetrable.[1] But if our faculty of knowledge is limited, our desire to know is unlimited. Just so far as to which this domain expands, and remains closed to the scientific

---

[1] [Arnold Toynbee has beautifully said that religion begins where the ocean of infinity beats on the shores of time.]

methods of observation and experience, the desire of
penetrating it survives and becomes even more in-
tense. It, therefore, addresses itself to religion and
its natural intuition; it demands most pressingly this
knowledge of perfection and the world beyond, which
science is unable to offer. So far from diminishing
the power of religion, science contributes rather to
its increase, enlarging the region open to it, but
closed to itself.

To this intellectual demand for knowledge concerning the world beyond must be added the needs of
feeling, which are the most imperious in our nature—
the need of loving a superior being, an ideal of power,
goodness, and beauty; the need of succour in adversity and suffering; the need of consoling oneself in
the present and hoping in the future. These needs
no physical or moral science can satisfy; religion
appeases, and can alone appease them. This is why
science cannot supersede religion, and why religion
will last as long as humanity itself endures. Everything induces us to believe that its *rôle* will be no less
important in the future than it has been in the past.
We may also conjecture that this utility will acquire
an extraordinary importance in the dangerous crisis
through which civilised societies are now passing.
This crisis will accomplish itself all the more speedily
if religion comes still further to aid science in undertaking the reform of individual "self-government"
and the collective government of society.[1]

[1] ["I do not hesitate to add that Socialism will either become
religious or cease to be." Comte d'Alveilla, *Hibbert Lectures*,
1891.]

CHAPTER XIII.

THE SOCIAL CRISIS.

THE progress of science and industry seems at the present day to be in a fair way to effect a revolution in the circumstances of the existence of society comparable only to that introduced by the discovery of edible herbs and the invention of agricultural implements. Thanks to the extraordinary increase in the productive and destructive powers of civilised man, the sphere of his liberty and security, which in old times never passed beyond the boundaries of his particular State, has extended itself over the greater part of the globe. The trade between nations which once amounted to millions has, after two or three centuries, risen to milliards. The circulation of labour and capital has also, little by little, become international. Hence, an extension corresponding to the joint responsibility for good and evil between members of the human family. When nations lived apart only unimportant ties existed, and these warfare made intermittent and precarious, and, consequently, the basis of security was cramped. People were interested in the affairs of their fellow-countrymen merely on account of the business transactions they performed with them. Again, there was a common interest in mutual defence from external at-

99

tacks, and in this defence each member of the State had to take his part. But there was no interest taken in the affairs of foreigners; it was rather their object to impoverish and weaken them in order to make them less terrible in battle. The solidarity of mankind stopped at the frontiers of the State.

The increasing and development of the exchange of all sorts of products, and the circulation of labour and of capital, has changed, and is still daily changing this state of things. We are interested in the prosperity of the nations with whom we do business just as they are interested in us, and we also suffer from injuries inflicted upon them. When the cotton crops begin to fail in the United States, hundreds of millions of European workers will be reduced to misery. When a crisis arises in Europe, it will have its echo throughout the rest of the world. In a word, the solidarity of good or evil fortune is universalised.

But good and evil fortunes do not depend simply on the environment in which man is placed, the nature of the soil, the accidents of climate; they also depend, perhaps even more powerfully, on his conduct, virtues, and vices. In proportion to the extension of this solidarity, the evil which it is in the power of vice to cause, the good which it is in the power of virtue to produce, will obtain greater scope. In the same way that a more perfect weapon can hit an object at a greater distance without losing its force of projection, so the maleficent influence of vice and the beneficent influence of virtue can increase in extent without weakening itself in the transit of so great a space.

This extension of the solidarity of human fortunes would perhaps have resulted in only salutary effects, if moral progress on the one side and economic on the other had gone along with industrial progress. Unfortunately, this has not been the case. Under the influence of progress in production and security, the ancient forms of individual protection, slavery, and serfdom have been abandoned, and the individual has become free. This new condition, giving him the right of self - government, but imposing on him responsibility for his destiny, has been a fertile source of both good and evil. He has been able to dispose of his labour, to turn his capacities to the best possible purposes, and obtain his share in the general increase of wealth. On the other hand, he has been under the necessity of providing for his own existence and that of his family, of rearing his children, and providing for his old age, and he has only been enabled to acquit himself of this necessity by rigorously restraining his appetite, by submitting to severe privations, and by foregoing the enjoyments of the present to secure the necessities of the future. It has been a dull and difficult task. Can the emancipated masses show themselves capable of undertaking it? Can they fulfil with exactitude the duties which self-government involves? Experience has too often witnessed their utter incapacity for self-rule.

While the increase in productive power multiplies riches, drunkenness, improvidence, sloth and neglect of family duties, add to the bulk of pauperism and the criminal classes. This is so, since the moral force re-

REESE LIBRARY
OF THE
UNIVERSITY
OF
CALIFORNIA.

quisite to the fulfilment of the duties entailed by
self-government is wanting to the masses set free
from their ancient serfdom.   At the same time,
the restraints of opinions and penal repression
have become relaxed.   The increasing facility for
getting out of the way has, on the one hand, diminished the efficacy of police supervision and the censure
of opinion, while, on the other, the penalties are miti-
gated without the repression of crime being ensured.

To the evils arising from the inadequacy of individual self-restraint are joined those of a collective
government which has ceased to be in keeping with
new conditions of social life.   We have described in
former publications the *rationale* of the political and
economic institutions of the old *régime*, and the
burdens they imposed upon the property and liberty
of individuals.   It was war that rendered these
necessary, and war in its turn was necessary in
order to secure civilisation.   The advance in the destructive power of civilised man by completely shelter-
ing civilisation from the attacks of the barbarian
world has done away with the necessary character
of warfare.   War has become an evil after having
originally been useful, and this is also true of the
political and economic institutions adapted to a
military era, and the burdens thereby imposed.
It has, therefore, been necessary, on the one side,
to establish a state of international peace, and,
on the other, to suppress the institutions and
encumbrances suited to a state of war—in other
words, to adapt the collective government of societies
to the new conditions dictated by the progress of

human powers of production and destruction. So
far from adopting such a line of conduct, what have
governments done ? They have artificially prolonged
the existence of the military stage, and have availed
themselves of the political and economic machinery,
which has been so adapted as to enable them to levy
an ever-increasing blackmail on the wealth extra-
ordinarily developed by modern methods of production. Such has been their intemperance that
they have increased their expenses more quickly than
their receipts. They have been compelled to increase
taxes, and in order to secure their acceptance, they
have had recourse to a double artifice. They have
been compelled to replace direct taxation, which
one sees, by indirect taxation, which one does
not see, and to associate in the profits of this governmental exploitation the more influential subjects,
landed proprietors, seats of industries, etc., thus making these, as it were, their accomplices in the spoliation of the masses. Yet not even these expedients
suffice to balance receipts with expenses. Recourse
has to be made to loans. Owing to the marvellous development of the methods of production, of saving and
credit, the civilised governments of the nineteenth
century have been able to increase their loans to such
an extent that they will bequeath to their successors
of the twentieth a debt already exceeding 120 milliards. Again, when we examine the use made of this
monstrous sum, we are bound to recognise that at
least nine-tenths of it has been dissipated in harmful
expenditure. From this it may be concluded that the
authors of this waste have perpetrated an act of

spoliation and theft against the future generations who must support the brunt of the interest and abatement of public debts.

Add together the evils arising from these two sources—the incapacity and inadequacy of individual self-government, and the intemperance and dishonesty of the public government, and you will arrive at a terrible result. If you consider how these evils have spread themselves throughout the extent of the civilised world, united as it is by the exchange of products and the loan of capital, you will explain to your satisfaction why the increase of wealth has not been accompanied by a corresponding increase in general well-being; you will understand the causes of the crisis through which society is now actually passing, a crisis which can but end one way if some restraint is not at an opportune moment brought to bear on this disastrous convulsion.

If well analysed, the causes of the social crisis are found to be primarily moral. Whence arises the incapacity and insufficiency of individual self-restraint? Whence but from the ignorance of the duties which the very term of "self-government" itself connotes, and from the absence of the moral force requisite to their accomplishment? Whence arises the intemperance and dishonesty of collective government? Whence but from the neglect of duties proper to this government, and the interests of egoists, who, blinded by their egoism, oppose themselves to the reforms necessary to adaptation to the new conditions of civilised social life?

Suppose, however, that the individual knows and

exactly fulfils all the duties necessitated by self-government ; that he is industrious, sober, temperate ; that he does not damage his health or diminish his forces by the immoderate satisfaction of animal appetites, the abuse of strong drink and sensual pleasures ; that he economises his actual consumption, in order to provide for his old age ; that he acquits himself punctually of his family duties; that he provides for their bodily and moral wants until they are of age to provide for themselves ; that he shows himself conscientious in the execution of his tasks if he is a worker ; that he refrains from abusing the misery and lack of foresight of his workers, snatching away the lion's share of toil, if he is an employer; that on every occasion he respects the good of others, and practises charity as far as his means will allow, if all these things represented actual facts, it is evident that humanity would find itself liberated from an enormous weight of evil. Suppose, again, that the class which governs society scrupulously fulfils the duties involved by this government ; that it takes as its rule the general interest of the nation ; that it allays rather than aggravates a state of militarism and protectionism, which has lost all justification ; that it only places on future generations the burden of expenses they will profit by; in a word, that it acquits itself of its governmental tasks with probity. In such a case we should be spared another feature of those evils from which we suffer, and which the increase of international solidarity tends to spread through all countries, despite the good or evil nature of their government. In short, supposing that these two govern-

ments—individual and social—were perfectly moral,
that all the duties they connote were correctly fulfilled,
the human species would only suffer from the evils
arising out of the imperfection and circumstances of
the environment in which it exists, and it would
advance without a disturbance at each increase in its
power of production.   In such a case, there would not
be to-day, nay, there would never have been, a social
crisis.

It is, then, a moral reform that must be accomplished in order to perfect either individual self-
government or collective government.   The necessary
agents of this double reform are Political Economy
and Religion.

CHAPTER XIV.

THE perfection of individual self-government and of collective government is dependent on two things :— (1) That the man who is to govern either himself or his fellows should know his duties ; (2) that he should possess the moral force necessary for their observance. If, on the other hand, we consider the immense majority of men, even in the most civilised countries, we find that they are but imperfectly cognisant of their duties, and we are even still more struck by the inadequacy of their moral capacity. As regards the duties of individual self-government, the practice and enlightenment of the age have doubtless imparted certain ideas to the people at large. Save, perhaps, in the lowest level of the population, everyone knows that he has duties to perform towards himself, towards his own family and his neighbour ; that he ought to provide subsistence for himself and his family ; that he ought to abstain from wronging his neighbour, and assist him in the hour of necessity. Everyone also knows that morality forbids him to abandon himself to idleness, to incontinence, to drunkenness, that is to say, to vices that place

107

an obstacle in the way of duty ; but these moral
notions are more or less scanty, and are rarely
reasoned out.

To turn to collective government, the recognition of
duty is even more confused and uncertain. In every
aggregation, whether a political society or nation, or an
industrial or commercial corporation, the governing
body has to undertake two sorts of duties—(1) towards
their society ; and (2) towards individuals or bodies
outside their pale. On the one side, rulers ought to
govern their own society in a manner conformable to
its interest, without being pre-occupied by their own ;
on the other, they ought to refrain from trenching
upon the property and liberty of other persons or
societies. Is it necessary to say that the notion of
duty is in either case obscured by the shadow cast
by particular or collective interests ?

There is, however, only a mere vague idea of the
evils which result from the utter neglect of duty,
evils which the extension of the sphere of human
solidarity has aggravated, evils which must insensibly
diminish the vital forces of the human species, and
detract from its capacity to fulfil the function assigned
it in the universal order. Insufficiency of knowledge as to what duty is, and of the evils which follow
its violation is the primary source of the imperfections and vices of collective and individual government. Their secondary source consists in the inadequacy of the moral force necessary in order to secure
the prevalence of duty over the individual interests
and passions that would infringe its laws.

We have already seen that, apart from religious

precept, the fulfilment of duty is determined by
motives of different sorts—the fear of legal penalties,
the desire of approbation and the fear of reprobation on the part of either one's fellows or one's
self, *i.e.* in the last case, conscience. To these
general motives must be added particular ones, such
as sentiments of affection for family and nation, and
the instinct of self-preservation. But these last do
not in themselves constitute a true morality, since
they often lead to the fulfilment of one duty by the
infraction of another. The paternal sentiment, for
instance, may drive the father of a family to improve
his fortune, *per fas et nefas.* So also the love of one's
folk or fatherland may, in international questions,
obscure the notions of justice and injustice. These
general motives possess, however, an assured efficacy
in no higher degree than the particular impulse of
altruistic or egoistic instincts. Penal repression is confined to the more serious infractions of rights or duty,
or to those which are so regarded : it does not apply
to a large number of immoral acts which it abandons
to the jurisdiction of opinion and the conscience. It is
subject to error, both as to the nature of the act which
it punishes (which, indeed, may not be punishable),
and as to the measure of the penalty. It is again
essentially uncertain in its application ; it may attack
the innocent and allow the guilty to escape. Opinion
has a sphere of action wider than legal penalties, but
it is too often vitiated by ignorance, interest or passion ; it approves things which it ought to blame, and
blames things which it ought to approve ; and lastly,
the increasing facility for getting about enables the

guilty to escape their penalty to-day with more ease
than was possible formerly. On the other hand, the
condemnation of one's own conscience cannot be
escaped. But does the conscience possess an assured
efficacy ? Are we certain that by listening to conscience we shall be able to govern not only ourselves,
but even others, in a manner most conformable to
the good of the species ?

The human soul possesses a feeling which answers to
justice and goodness, to which an unjust or evil act
causes pain, a good and just act pleasure ; this
is the moral sense. But the moral sense does
not sit in judgment ; it rather receives the judgment which the conscious intelligence or the conscience passes upon an act. Again, conscience is
not infallible, and if a proof is needed, it suffices
to instance the fallibility of the public conscience,
which is but the aggregation of individual con-
sciences. The conscience cannot deceive itself upon
the nature of an act, so as to esteem an unjust and
evil act good and equitable, to satisfy or arouse the
moral sense by a conscious lie. It can, however,
only judge sanely on condition of its being enlightened, and this is far from being generally
the case.[1] But if this is the case, the verdict

[1] [This is to say that the conscience is supreme, not that it is
infallible. Principal Fairbairn has taken Cardinal Newman to
task for holding, as his two main principles, the probability of
knowledge and the supremacy of conscience. This is a mistake,
but it is only important here to distinguish between the
supremacy of conscience and its infallibility. The first is consistent with any theory of knowledge, the latter hardly consistent with facts.]

ought without fail to be immediately executed. Yet this cannot happen unless the conscience has at its call a force strong enough to assure the execution. If, for instance, a particular judge is covetous of another's property, it is necessary that his conscience should be fortified with a force sufficient to surmount the efforts of the interest and passion which lead him to possess himself of this property in the face of the law.

On the one hand, then, it is necessary in order that the conscience should be enlightened, that it should know how to discern good from evil, what is conformable from what is contrary to duty ; on the other, it must be armed with a moral force, which will enable it to break down the resistance which self-seeking and passion oppose to the fulfilment of duty.

To enlighten the conscience is the business of Political Economy. To arm the conscience is the business of Religion.

CHAPTER XV.

RIGHTS and duties form the subject matter of morals. Rights define the limits of individual and social property and liberty; duties prescribe the profitable usage of property and liberty within their respective limits. Rights and duties are enjoined by laws, manners, and customs. In the earliest times, as we have seen, the laws which each society observed were revealed by the gods to their ministers, magicians, oracles, or prophets. Some of these laws concerned individual government, others collective government, but all equally had in view the good of society, and for this very reason were accepted and obeyed. When they ceased to have this object in view, society addressed itself to other gods who revealed to it other laws. In course of time a separation was made between religion and the State. This separation also extended itself to the sphere of morals. The State possessed the code which it had inherited from the legislation of religion, but here, in accordance with changes effected in the existence of society, the lay jurists and administrators completed a gradual reform. Religion, on its side, maintained its code of laws,

which the doctors and casuists undertook to revise
and supplement, when the older laws no longer re-
sponded to the contemporary state of opinion. Each
society had, then, two codes of law—the code of the
State authorised by the machinery of coercion, and the
code of religion authorised by the punishments and rewards which the State was able respectively to accord
or deny. While religion remained united to the State,
despite the separation of civil from religious functions,
the two codes remained very much the same. Differences, however, grew up, and these became accentuated
when, the tribal gods having given place to universal
gods like those of Buddhism and Christianity, the
frontiers of religion and the State ceased to be the
identical.

The aim of the State code was State interest.
Besides the definition and demarcation of rights
and duties of personal and general government, it
comprised a whole series of obligations, some necessitated by the incapacity of the masses to profit by
their rights and fulfil their natural or conventional
duties, some by the exigencies of personal and general
security necessitating the subordination of the rights
and duties of individuals to the welfare of the State.
But everything not directly concerned with the
maintenance of internal order and external security,
the State passed over in its code, and these things religion included in its code. At first religious morality,
as it was elaborated by the doctors and casuists of
Christianity, comprised with a few points of difference the same laws as figured in the State code, excepting only those which could only be applied to

members of the nation ; at a later date it included a whole body of rules concerned with the special duties due to the Church, together with the rights and duties the State had deemed it unnecessary to enrol and confirm in its code. These rights and duties, unrecognised by the State, religion defined and caused to be observed. In violating them, one committed not a crime or delict, but a " sin."

So long as Church and State remained associated, and the two codes distinct, the Church, save in those rare cases when the two systems were mutually opposed, ratified the civil code, and the State in its turn sanctioned those portions of the religious in which the Church claimed the aid of the secular arm, the payment of tithes, the interdiction of heresies, etc. But in either case, as has been well remarked, the aim of both the civil and the religious law was, "utility" — utility or the interest of religion including the interest of the faithful, and the utility or interest of the State under which was included that of its subjects. The obedience which the faithful subjects accorded these laws was always proportioned to the utility they attributed to them. When an advance in either the governing capacities of individuals, or the security of society diminished the utility of certain institutions, such, for instance, as slavery, or rendered them harmful, the obedience to the civil laws maintaining these institutions became weakened, and a crisis set in until these institutions and laws became amenable to the new conditions. It was the same with religious laws, although from their very nature they were slower in readapting themselves.

This survey of the rights and duties which furnish the unchanging and universal element of morality and the obligations which form its changeable and relative element, furnishes an explanation of the present crisis. The increase in the productive and destructive powers of civilised man has altered the conditions of personal and social life. Obligations once so necessary have now become injurious. Such has become the political subjection whose *raison d'être* has disappeared with the secured preponderance of the civilised over the barbarian world ; such, again, has been the personal subjection, slavery and serfdom, which, by preserving a voluntary tutelage over the masses of incapables, we might have suppressed without thrusting compulsory "self - go-vernment" on reluctant persons. It is from the suppression of all personal tutelage together with the maintenance of political incapacity that the present crisis has sprung. To seek out the causes which have occasioned it, to make an inventory of the evils it has produced and continues to produce, such is the task assigned to Political Economy, the science of the useful. It may be formulated as follows. *In that which concerns " self-government,"* to record the losses of vital force, and the suffer-ing caused by the vices of the government, the attacks on the property and liberty of others, breaches of duty towards self and towards those for whom we are re-sponsible, intemperance under its diverse forms, drunkenness and incontinence ; to estimate the extent of the injury done by attacks on rights, and the breach of duties throughout the community, peoples whose commerce has been consolidated; to point out the remedies for the vices of self-government; and to establish for persons unable to bear the responsibility inseparable from liberty, a tutelage adapted to the degree of their intellectual and moral development. *In that which concerns collective government,* to record the evils caused by the vices and wrongful extension of this government, the gross imperfection in its duties, the privileges it has conferred on the influential at the expense of the people, the damaging enterprises, which, through withholding from the public its rights of discussion, it has embarked nations against their will — in short, to draw up the indictment of militarism, protectionism, autocracy, to point out the reforms necessary in a collective government which has ceased to be *en rapport* with society and also the best method of effecting these reforms. To enlighten conscience upon the score of nuisances caused by the wrongs and imperfections of individual and general government, to discover the remedies—this, in short, is the rôle of Political Economy.

But will a mere enlightenment of the conscience suffice to compel either the individual or the rulers to reform their government ? No. It is also necessary that the moral force opposed to the allurements of selfish passions and interests should be armed with power sufficient for the purpose. This moral armament of the conscience is the province of religion.

NOTE.—Must morality be classified among the sciences or simply among the arts ? This vexed question is easily settled if we distinguish the mutable and immutable elements in rights and duties. These two things form the matter of morality.

(See Molinari: *La Morale Economique and Notions Fonda-mentales d'Economie Politique.*) Rights are constituted by property and liberty in their natural limits. Duty is the use to which each ought to put his property and liberty within the limits defined by right. It is pretended that the limits of property and liberty are not defined by nature, and that there are no such things as "Natural Rights," and that, therefore, it belongs to legislators, lawyers, or doctors to fix these limits, and enjoin their practice with a view to the changing state of society. From this it would appear that morality is nothing more than the art of legislators, doctors, jurists—the art of perfecting rights and duties in their relation to the varying needs of society. Such a thesis, if true, would imply nothing short of the spoliation of the individual with a view to subjecting his property and liberty to the tender mercies of legislators, jurists and doctors, and would make straight the path of communism.

It is necessary to show all this to be false, that everyone possesses by nature his own powers, and is free to enjoy the property acquired by the useful employment of his faculties, that his liberty and property have their *natural* limitations in the liberty and property of others, that each has his *natural* duties to fulfil, on the one hand, duties of parents to children, duties of children to parents, etc. etc., and, on the other, conventions, obligations, etc., which bind everyone to direct his property and liberty to the fulfilment of these obligations.

In what, then, consists the art of legislators, jurists, and doctors? It consists in distinguishing the limits of property and liberty, and of securing them within these limits, in distinguishing natural duties and conventional obligations, and causing the limits of freedom and property to be known. Rights and duties remain the same at all times and in all places —immutable and universal. It is the capacity for practising them that varies; it is the means by which their exercise is assured that alter. It is the "obligations" which are essentially relative to time and place, which have as their *raison d'être* the inadequacy of capacity and security, and which vary with these last. If we all were able to make full advantage of our

REESE LIBRARY
OF THE
UNIVERSITY
OF
CALIFORNIA

property and liberty, there would have been no necessity to subject the incapable to voluntary or compulsory tutelage.   If everyone had spontaneously and without any external constraint, respected the rights of others, and fulfilled his natural and conventional obligations, no apparatus of defence would have been necessary to assure social security, nor would it have been necessary, from time to time, to establish and modify personal obligations.   In such a case the art of legislators, lawyers, and doctors would have been useless.

In short, morality contains natural and immutable elements (which are rights and duties), and artificial and mutable elements (which are obligations).   The knowledge of these twofold elements is a science ; their application is an art.

CHAPTER XVI.

WHEN the conscience has pronounced her verdict upon
the good or evil, useful or harmful, moral or immoral
character of an act, she appeals for the force necessary
for the execution of her sentence to the law of
justice and goodness, the hatred of injustice and
wickedness that exists in every mind, that is to say,
the moral sense. This sense, however, like all its
companions, exists in very diverse degrees of perfection.
In a great number of persons it has only reached the
embryonic state ; in others, if more developed, it is as
yet only able to oppose an insufficient resistance to
the appetites and passions which thwart the execution
of the verdict of conscience. In such cases, it is
necessary to have recourse, either to coercion, to the fear
of pain, and the desire of public approbation, or else to
the fear of chastisement and the hope of reward held out
by religion. In the natural aristocracy of humanity
the moral sense is adequate to its task, and needs no
auxiliary ; the individual does good and abstains from
evil without considering chastisements or recompenses
in this world or any other. But need we state that
this aristocracy is very small, and that so great is the

infirmity of human nature, that even the best men
are not always able by pure moral force to surmount
the vicious inclinations, appetites, interests, or passions? Each victory these foes win over duty,
each defeat of the conscience, causes a loss of moral
force, a weakening of the moral sense. Should the
conscience be but insufficiently fortified, she will find
support in either active coercion, public opinion,
or religion, but of these three factors of morality,
religion alone possesses an assured efficacy and irresistible force.

We do not forget that human actions are, in
ultimate analysis, always determined by motives of
pain and pleasure. Yet if the satisfaction procur-
able by the fulfilment of duty were inferior to that
afforded by the vicious forces, where would the
victory be? Whatever the religious idea may be,
religion alone is able to place in the foreground
of duty a satisfaction or a penalty always in excess of
the enjoyment procured by an immoral satisfaction.
If the idea is that of paganism, if the individual in
surmounting his appetites or passions, in order to
fulfil a duty he believes to be prescribed by the Deity,
is obedient merely to a fear of chastisement, and
the hope of a reward, this chastisement or reward possesses none the less in his eyes a character of certainty
or infinity which is totally absent from the punishments and rewards of the penal code or of public
opinion. If the idea is that of Christianity, and if
the believer is obedient to his love for a Being who
is infinitely powerful as he is also just and good,
he will also derive from this feeling an assured satis-

faction superior to all the enjoyments of this world. According to this conception, we do our duty or overcome our passions not simply to escape a punishment or obtain a recompense, but to obey our religious sense of God-given love, reverence, and fear. But why do we experience this feeling? Why do we love God? We love him on account of His attributes of power, justice, goodness, by which it is His to recompense the good and to punish the evil. If, therefore, we do good or abstain from evil, not simply in order to obtain a reward or avoid a penalty, that is to say for an interested end, but if we are obedient to a feeling of love mingled with fear and reverence, this sentiment is in ultimate analysis, none the less, founded upon the power attributed to God of distributing to His creatures an eternity of joy or woe, of pain or of pleasure. This is a sentiment analogous to that of loyalty to the old monarchies. The king was loved with a disinterested love, but the cause of this love was the unlimited power by which an absolute monarch is able to reward or punish, to make or mar, to raise or put down, to enrich or ruin the power, in short, of procuring for his subjects sensations of pleasure or inflicting on them those of pain.

Religion appears, then, as a necessary agent, and as the sole absolutely efficacious one, in the development and preservation of the moral sense. This is the part it is called upon to play at the present day in the existing crisis. The present crisis, as we have seen, arises, on the one hand, from the insufficiency of personal self-government, on the other, from the incapacity of the majority to fulfil the duties involved in

the responsibility inseparable from liberty; from the imperfection and backward state of collective government,
the harmful, and often the immoral employment, on
the part of the governing classes, of the power placed
in their hands by the preservation of an obsolete
political bondage.   In order to remedy the ills of
this twofold 'government and the evils which spring
from it, it is necessary, as we have also seen, to enlighten the conscience as to the beneficial or evil,
moral or immoral elements in the government of self,
as well as the institutions and practices of collective government.   This is the business of Political
Economy.

It is also necessary to arm the conscience with a
moral force powerful enough to effect the reform
of these two governments.   This is the work of
Religion.

The accomplishment of this work, in its turn, involves—first, the spread of the faith in the masses
of those who govern themselves, and, *à fortiori*, in
those who govern others besides themselves ; and
secondly, the application to moral reform of the power
which religious faith alone can supply.   To cause faith
to penetrate souls, and to place it at the service of
the government of self and others, such is the task
which, nowadays, more than ever, is incumbent on religion.   Will existing religions fulfil this task ?   What
at the present moment is the state of religious and
moral culture in countries belonging to our civilisation ?
These are questions which must be next examined.

CHAPTER XVII.

IT is necessary to state that, upon the actual conditions of religious culture, we have but vague and
conjectural data. Of all branches of human activity,
religion is perhaps the one upon which we possess
the least complete and least trustworthy evidence.
Statistics of all sorts—agricultural, industrial, financial—increase annually; detailed returns of foreign
trade are published; commissions are set on foot with
prolix inquiries concerning the state of different
branches of production, the relations of capital and
labour, etc. etc. We are enabled to collect positive
and more or less accurate information upon the state
of population, public and private wealth, crime, education, and to say whether civilised nations have
progressed or retrogressed between any given points
of time. Nothing like this exists in the case of religion. We possess, indeed, lists of religions and existing sects, we are acquainted with their geographical
distribution, and nominally, at least, with the number
of their adherents; we have also data concerning
their ministers and their property, balance sheets

relative to clerical emoluments; but these statistics[1] are most inadequate, and do not afford any precise idea of actual religious conditions.

Yet, it is none the less apparent that religious culture is insufficient and backward even in those countries where, at first sight, it would seem to be most highly developed and its supporters most numerous. Religion, like society itself, is undergoing a crisis, and this crisis is for the most part, if not entirely, due to the false and uncertain position in which it has been placed—more especially in Catholic countries—by the rupture of the State alliance having been effected without any due security and liberty being given in exchange.

In the countries where, up till the last century, Catholicism has possessed a monopoly, the clergy, unconsoled for its loss, are compelled to attempt its reconquest. It has, in France, Belgium, Germany, taken an active part in political struggles; the priest having donned the rôle of politician, has transferred to the conflicts of rival parties the passion and intolerance peculiar to religious warfare. We cannot in fairness blame him for this. The tendency to monopoly is essentially human—it characterises the agriculturist who, in like manner, pretends to the exclusive power of providing the needs of the whole body, as well as the priest who wishes to appropriate to himself the salvation of the soul, and to exclude all rival claimants. The clergy,

[1] [As an example of this we cannot forbear from instancing the contradictory statistics brought forward to prove the numerical preponderance of non-conformity in Wales.]

moreover, are able to claim an excuse which protectionist merchants and landlords cannot—*viz.* that up till the present they have had no other alternative between governing themselves and being oppressed. For, while the adversaries of landed and commercial monopolies wish merely to reduce the monopolies by ordinary rights of property and liberty, the adversaries of the clergy aim at placing them outside this common right by limiting their freedom of association and possession, taxing their property, restricting their liberty of instruction, and obliging those who receive their instruction to contribute to the expenses of the official instruction which they do not receive. In taking part in political questions, and placing their influence on the side of a party, the clergy has only submitted to an imperious necessity—a necessity which has in turn called forth revolutionary intolerance.

" Clericalism," or the alliance of religion and politics, is in no less degree detrimental to the clergy whom it demoralises and whose religion it discredits. By abandoning themselves to politics, by interfering in elections, by intriguing for the prostitution of government to their own exclusive interests, the clergy have not only neglected the matters which ought to constitute their sole business—the religious and moral life of their folk, but have also contracted the immoral habits, and vicious practices inherent in statecraft, lying, intimidation, and corruption. Religion has naturally suffered from the negligence and debasement of its ministers. It has lost its influence, and given ground to the Radicals who wish to suppress and supersede it.

Religious institutions are, therefore, in a position analogous to that of political and economic institutions. Just as Conservatives pretend, some that there is nothing in the *status quo* needing modification, others that it is necessary to revive the *status quo ante*, so Socialists and Anarchists of all sorts are unanimously of opinion that it is necessary to destroy the old society, and in its place build up an entirely new social edifice.[1] In other words, Conservatives do not wish to acknowledge the evils that it is their duty to cure; Socialists, who acknowledge these evils, and have a natural tendency to exaggerate them, propose a remedy calculated to kill rather than cure. In like way, in religious matters, the spirit of negation or of *Utopia* has to contend almost alone with the spirit of conservatism, or, to speak more plainly, routine.

The philosophers in the last century, and the freethinkers, their heirs in this, have declared war with all established religions in general, and Catholicism in particular, and this by either denying the existence of God, or by disengaging the " Supreme Being " from the ancient religious conceptions, and inventing for His use new modes of worship. The more or less scientific negations of materialism and atheism, which have left the masses without provision for their religious needs, have not as yet passed beyond the threshold of the guest chambers of free thought. Some of their adepts, at whose head Auguste Comte[2] must be mentioned,

---

[1] [This would not necessarily be true of our English school of opportunist Socialists.]

[2] [Comte cannot be fairly described by the English term

perceiving that these needs must be satisfied, have desired to replace the religion of God by that of Humanity.

But if humanity has its virtues, it also has its im-- perfections, weaknesses, coarse appetites, and vices. As we have said elsewhere in an appreciation of Comte's doctrine, we might just as well adore some useful animal—the calf Apis, for instance.[1] Despite the high opinion of himself which a human being usually cherishes, the masses refuse to adore him. Ridicule may do ample justice to the Religion of Humanity. The worship of the "Supreme Being" does not incur these objections; since all religions, excepting the lowest forms of fetichism, have practised this worship from times immemorial, and have accumulated a capital of observation and experience which enables them to adapt it to the intelligence and feelings of their faithful. They have rendered the divine ideal accessible and intelligible; they have discovered the ways by which this idea may reach and penetrate souls. Whenever anyone has attempted to replace their historical dogmas and ceremonial by impro-

"atheist." He was rather an agnostic, who, thinking that man- kind would pass from a metaphysical to a positive stage, wished to substitute a "Religion of Humanity" for that of the "Unknow- able," whose existence as such, he contended, could not affect man's rational action.]

[1] *Cf.* an article by M. Molinari in the *Journal Des Economistes*, Oct., 1891, entitled "Le Postivism on la Doctrine Sociale de M. Auguste Comte," R. P. Grueber. [See also *Auguste Comte : Sa Vie et Sa Doctrine;* Ed. Caird, *Social Philosophy of Auguste Comte;* and Bishop Westcott, *Gospel of the Resurrection.* Ap- pendixes.]

visations, he has failed completely. Indeed, attempts
to modify formalism and venerable rites have been
rarely successful. An instance of such an attempt is
the substitution in Catholic worship of the vulgar for
the dead Latin language. The words of a service do
not, however, derive their value from their literal sense,
but from their capacity to arouse and satisfy religious feeling.

Progress in religion does not, therefore, consist in
suppressing existing forms of worship, in depriving
religious needs of their food, or in replacing the adoration of a divine being infinitely above man by the
idolatry of humanity; much less does it consist in
inventing in all points a new system of worship. We
can doubtless imagine new conceptions of God, or of the
universe and its government, or of man and his destiny ;
but these conceptions, however they may be formed,
cannot be based upon sure and certain ideas. For in
even a smaller degree than supernatural communications, which reveal to man the secret of his destiny,
and give him the answer to the enigma of the universe—admitting that he possesses the necessary
faculties for the comprehension of this answer—
religious innovations, seductive as they may be, will
remain confined to the domain of the imagination.
The old religions, it may be, are founded on legends,
but new ones can but be founded on guesses, and
legends are, at least, authenticated by the tradition
and lapse of time. Moreover, the religions and the
sects of the world are to be counted by millions.
Would it not be but a meagre progress to invent one
more ?

In what, then, does religious progress consist, if it does not consist in inventing new religions? We must now address ourselves to find an answer to this problem.

REESE LIBRARY
OF THE
UNIVERSITY
OF
CALIFORNIA.

CHAPTER XVIII.

If we are desirous of describing the probable future of religion, we must first find out the nature of its progress in the past. In its origin, and even still among savage folk grown old in a long infancy, religious feeling is aroused by the appearance of natural phenomena, which determine the formation of religion. Religion is a complex feeling in which the primary element is reverence for force, and a feeling such as a frail creature, conscious of his frailty, experiences when in the presence of a being endowed with superior strength—a dwarf in the presence of a giant. To this reverence inspired by a superior force, is added a feeling of love or fear, proportioned to the measure in which this powerful being shows himself benevolently or malevolently disposed.

The primitive man, in the presence of nature, found himself as a dwarf in the presence of a giant. In the unexplored environment in which he was cast, he witnessed the action of a host of phenomena, some causing sensations of pleasure, others sensations of pain or unhappiness. These things, which he himself was unable to effect, the heat and light of the

130

sun, the alteration of day and night, rain, thunder, pestilence, etc., have, however, a cause; they are produced by an agent. This cause, this agent, manifestly provided with a greater power than man's, directs and sets at work the machinery of nature. It remains invisible like the machinist behind scenery, but its existence is attested by these displays of activity. The imagination of primitive man represented it under forms appropriate to its beneficent or maleficent works, and his plastic aptitude materialised these forms in idols. In the imagination of this child-man, the idol became pregnant with life, the invisible spirit dwelt there, and communicated itself to objects put in touch with it. Hence fetiches and amulets. This is the religious conception in its rudimentary state.

Such a conception engenders a worship suited to the nature of the powerful beings that produce occurrences useful or the reverse for man. Can man possibly conceive of these beings as different from himself, obeying other motives, animated by other passions, experiencing other needs? It is necessary, then, if one wishes to attract their favour and disarm their wrath, to comport one's self towards them as one would comport one's self towards men endowed with greater power. It is necessary to provide for their wants, and obey their orders. It is necessary to lodge, dress, deck, nourish the idols in which they are embodied as sumptuously and abundantly as possible, and to address prayers and homage to them analogous to those paid to human potentates. This is the cult, and it is suited to the nature, character and function of the divine being dwelling in the idol.

The man who believes most firmly in the existence of these idol-enshrined gods, who experiences in the presence of the idols a feeling of reverence, fear or love, *i.e.* a religious feeling, cannot fail to consult and demand from them rules of conduct. When this consultation takes place under circumstances of great mystery, in the midst of the dark recesses of a cavern, such as the cave of the Sibyl, or better still, on the top of a mountain, in the gleams of lightning as at Sinai, the spirit makes answer; it dictates the law which must be adopted, the conduct which must be followed. This response attributed to the Deity is nothing else than the expression of the thought of the man who consulted the oracle under the excitement of religious feeling—just as in the modern spiritualist superstition, the answer of the spirits is nothing but the reverberation of the medium's thoughts. The efficacy of the law so formed, and dictated by the Deity, is in proportion to faith in the power of this Deity, and the sentiment of reverence, love, or fear. Such is the feeling generated by the character, and developed by the worship of idols who have become the creators and preservers of the rules of conduct observed by the individual and by the petty society, herd, class, or tribe of which he is a member.

Such is the religious conception of the primitive idolaters. We already find here, although in an embryonic state, the constituent data of all religions:

1. The existence of superior powers who are the causes and agents of natural phenomena.

2. The necessity incumbent on man to worship these powers by fashioning a body in which they may dwell, just as the spirit of man dwells in his own body, and by lodging, clothing, and feeding this idol to render it propitious.

3. The necessity of consulting these superior powers in order to know their desires and will, and to demand from them rules of conduct which must be followed individually and socially.

4. The law they inspire or dictate, and the authority they bring to its acceptance.

This conception developed and rounded itself off up to a certain point in the religions of the nations who, upon the discovery of edible herbs and the invention of the early arts, superseded the tribes. It was in such a way that paganism with its hierarchy and division of official labour, constituted itself on all sides, and that the relations of subjection of each people, city or nation, with this government, the tributes to be paid, the consultations to be made, and the means of obtaining them through the agencies of sibyls, augurs, etc., came to be defined. But at least in the world of our civilisation, it was necessary that Christianity should come, in order that a decisive progress in the religious conception might be achieved.

This progress consisted primarily in a radical change in the relationship of God and man. The gods of . paganism, as well as the spirits of idolatry and fetichism, were actuated by personal interest; they protected their people, but only on condition of a tribute paid them as a rent from tenants; they rendered them services, but this was on condition of

K

remuneration. In the room of these lazy and avaricious beings, Christianity enthroned a disinterested God, whose relations with man were not those of a proprietor or master with his slaves or tenants, but those of a father with his children. The motive He follows is not that of self-interest, but love, and this love He extends to a sublime sacrifice. He exacts no tribute for enjoyment of his domain, no payment for the services He renders and the favours he accords ; all that he asks of man is to love Him as a father, and, in his own interest, to obey His law. This law, revealed by Himself, He has authorised by re-- warding those who observe it, and punishing those who infringe it. Thus if God considers and treats men as His children, and not as slaves or subjects, the feelings of man to Him ought to undergo a like change ; man ought to love Him as a father, and this love ought naturally to surpass in elevation and energy the love that a slave or serf evinces for his master. The love of God—for such is the result of the Christian concept—is a feeling incomparably stronger than any feeling derived from paganism, and becomes in consequence a more powerful and efficacious instrument for the observation of the law.

This religious concept has already existed for nineteen centuries ; it has been adopted by the people who constitute the flower of humanity ; and during this long period the human mind has imagined nothing that can better respond to its highest aspirations. We do not mean to say that the religious condition of Christian peoples has been susceptible of no advance ; that the four hundred and seventy-

seven millions of persons whom statisticians classify
under the different denominations of Christendom are
equally imbued with the divine love ; that this love is
in their midst equally pure, and has sufficient power
to restrain the vicious or excessive appetites and passions militating against the preservation of the moral
law, or that this law is in entire harmony with new
conditions of social life.   No, in these different respects
the religious condition of peoples called Christian is
singularly imperfect—perhaps even retrograde.   The
difference in religions is perhaps more general than it
has ever been before ; the instrument supplied by religion for the fulfilment of the law is perhaps even less
effective.   Yet this state of things cannot be remedied
by making a clean sweep of the religions of the past,
and the substitution of some new invention, as the
revolutionists of 1793 and their successors have desired
to do.   It can, in fact, only be remedied by extending
religious culture, by adapting it to the mental state of
the people, by strengthening, and, when necessary,
reforming the existing law.

Under the present state of things, religious culture
leaves vast extents uncultivated.   There are but few
men who are naturally and completely atheists, who
have not a germ of religious feeling, in whom this
germ cannot be developed by an education suited to
their mental condition.   But we can affirm with certainty that in the countries where religions are State-
subsidised, and where the clergy form a mere body of
officials, this education is neglected.[1]   Supplied with

---

[1] M. Taine has attempted to account for the actual state of
religious life among Catholics.   He affirms that in France, and

an assured minimum of the means of existence, the clergy fail to take the necessary efforts to increase their flock, and bring the indifferent to the practice of religion. In countries where this practice is rendered obligatory, it usually degenerates into a lifeless formalism. If the observation of those rites, which experience leads us to recognise as best calculated to arouse and develop in souls the feeling of a divine love, is an indispensable factor, it nevertheless is not all sufficient; it must be supported by precept and example. It is necessary that the pastor should take pains to enunciate his religious and moral ideas. It is also necessary that he himself should possess faith in the mission entrusted to him, and that his conduct should be in harmony with his teaching, for otherwise his teaching will be vain. Lastly, it is necessary that the religious and moral ideas ministered to by

particularly in Paris, there is a tremendous difference between the nominal and effective body of supporters of Catholicism. According to Mr. T. W. Allies' *Journal of a Visit to France*, "M. Dufresne (July, 1845) told us that out of a million inhabitants of Paris, it has been estimated that 300,000 go to Mass, and 50,000 are *Chrétiens pratiquants*." (Conversation with the Abbé Petitot, curé of Saint Louis d'Antin, 7th July, 1847.) "Of thirty-two million French folk, but two millions go to Confession." To-day (April, 1890) an eminent and well informed ecclesiastic writes to me, "As a rough estimate, I should think that about 100,000 persons made their Easter Communion in Paris." The numbers differed much in various parishes. Madeleine, 4500 out of 29,000 inhabitants; St. Augustin, 6500 out of 29,000; St. Eustache, 17,500 out of 20,000; Billancourt, 500 out of 10,000; Grenella, 1500 out of 47,000; Belleville, 1500 out of 60,000. At Paris, out of 100 children, 24 are unbaptised. *Cf.* Taine's *La Reconstruction de la France en 1800. Revue des Deux-Mondes*, June 1st, 1891.

the rites of worship should be adapted to the mental condition of the individuals, in whom it is necessary to awaken and develop the feeling of the divine love.

In this respect what is true of artistic education is true of religious education. It must, under the penalty of becoming abortive, be graduated and proportioned to the capacity of those to whom it is given. A madonna of Raphael, or a symphony of Beethoven will fail to impress the savage whose artistic cravings are completely satisfied by a coarse daub or the violent beating of a gong. This feeling can only be developed and refined by a lengthy education, and even this alone will not suffice, but must be assisted by a general cultivation of the intellect. In the same way, the majority, not merely of savages, but even of civilised people, are not able to elevate themselves up to a purely immaterial and ideal conception of the Deity. It needs must be embodied in idols and represented by images, and if we were to penetrate into the souls of these masses, we should doubtless make strange discoveries there. We should find that this conception hardly differs in form from that of paganism. But is this to declare it necessary that we should, after the manner of the Protestant sects, do away with these idols images, relics, charms, etc.? No, for so far from rekindling religious feeling, this would only serve to extinguish and deprive it of the moral force, weak and crude as it may be, which it brings to the service of duty.[1] It is necessary rather to place before it such

[1] On the attempt to christianise Africa ; cf. Jules Vinson, *Les Religions Actuelles*, p. 335 ; and R. Hartmann, *Les Peuples de L'Afrique*, p. 173. But would Christianity, if not put for-

a conception of the Deity as it has the capacity to attain to. Again, it must be remarked that religious education does not in itself suffice to realise this advance, which is, in fact, dependent on the general progress, and notably on the progress of industrial machinery, which develops intellectual faculties by elevating the nature of the work necessitated by the national demand for the means of existence.[1]

To extend and modify religion in such a way as to propagate and elevate the instinct of divine love, and in consequence to develop the force that this feeling brings to the support of the trials of life and the fulfilment of duty—this is the first advance that we have to realise. But this advance alone will not suffice. Religious feelings may be applied to good and evil ends alike. Associated with the worst traits of our nature, with avarice, cruelty, the spirit of monopoly, it may become a terrible agent of destruction, the abettor of most outrageous crimes. It inspired the revocation of the "Edict of Nantes," and the massacre of the unoffending peoples of the New World. It is necessary to direct and confine it to its natural end, which is to assist in fulfilment of duty. Duty is no light task; instincts and passions of formidable power must be struggled with—egotism,

ward in all its purity, be preferable to the gross fetichism of the natives? The Jesuits have well understood that it is often necessary to bring religion down to the level of uncultured souls almost bordering on bestiality. The success of their mis· sion in Paraguay was due to the application of this principle. They may perhaps have abused it, but were they altogether wrong in using it?

[1] See Molinari : *Cours d'Economie Politique*, lesson viii.

carnal appetites, covetousness of another's goods; we must make self-sacrifices which involve painful privations. This direction of religious feeling is no less than religious culture within the province of the clergy. They ought to devote themselves to understanding the condition of souls, to appreciating in each case the force which may be set to work in the service of duty, and the degree of the power possessed by appetites needing control and regulation. According to circumstances, they ought to refuse or allow moral concessions, contenting themselves with a half-victory, when a complete one is impossible. But here again, need we say, they show themselves inadequate to their task, and contribute even less to the direction of religious feeling than they do to its birth and growth? The proof of this the fact lies in insufficient influence of religion upon the conduct of the individual, and the slight difference we can observe between the morality of those who practice religion and that of those who do not. There is perhaps even more advance to be made in the application of the religious sentiment to the fulfilment of law than in the cultivation of this feeling itself.

Another advance consists in the harmonising of religious codes with the everchanging circumstances of social life. These codes, which contain a collection of political, moral, and hygienic rules or prescriptions, now superannuated, have, in other respects, also become inadequate and incomplete, since they do not take into account the new circumstances to which economic progress has given birth.

These, then, are the points at which progress touches

upon religion.   This progress, which goes on incessantly—and is to be traced throughout the whole of
human history, may be accomplished with greater or
less speed, according to the circumstances in which
religion finds its place.   Like material progress, religious progress presupposes certain conditions which
may be summed up in two words — property and
liberty.

CHAPTER XIX.

THE faculties of the soul, like the physical forces, require their special kinds of sustenance. If this is refused, or but insufficiently afforded, they decline and perish ; if it is granted in sufficient quantity, they survive and develop. Agriculture, fishing, the chase, etc., provide for the bodily needs ; religion, the fine arts, science, nourish in their proper sphere the moral forces. The same rule applies to the moral as well as the physical forces. The branches of human industry which supply their necessities exact an application, more or less considerable, of capital and labour, as well as the co-operation of a body of workers and the acquisition of materials. Religious needs do not escape this common necessity. All religions, save those of peoples excessively poor, are served by a special staff of ministers, and possess a stock of movable and immovable property, churches, statues, images, ornaments, seminaries, convents, libraries, etc. It is necessary to collect such a *personnel*, and the material stock must be found and preserved in such a condition as to provide for the requirements of worship. It is necessary to recruit and prepare the

141

clergy, to construct and ornament churches or temples, to minister to the expense of religious ceremonies, etc. etc. These items vary with the different religions. The Catholic demands a more considerable stock of materials than the Protestant; but, on the other hand, the maintenance of a celibate clergy is less costly than that of a married. Although, in this respect, statistics only afford us with an insufficient evidence, it is apparent that in all civilised countries, ecclesiastical establishments represent a great deal of capital and a great annual expenditure. Under the old *régime* this capital was principally furnished by donations, and the annual expenses were met by the tithe and alms. For these revenues, a State-paid salary has been substituted, and the maintenance of places of worship, which has been made a charge on the State budget, has been placed under the jurisdiction and province of a minister of public worship. The vices of this system, that transforms religion into a mere branch of the administration, have become apparent, and to-day there is an ever increasing movement of opinion towards the separation of Church and State. The natural consequence of such a separation would be the concession to the clergy of the right of freely organising themselves under the form of one or several corporations, of administering their own affairs in their own way, and without any interference on the part of the State, of acquiring and possessing, without any limits in extent or duration, movable or immovable property, of collecting subscriptions, and of fixing at their own tariff the prices of its offices. These conditions the promoters and partisans of the separation always refuse to recognise. They dread, or profess to dread, the return of the characteristic abuses of the old ecclesiastical *régime*, the monopolising of the soil, the reconstruction of a priestly caste which, they say, would subjugate civil society by its influence, etc. etc. But would these abuses and perils—real indeed when the established religion was in possession of a monopoly secured by Draconian penalties—be able to re-appear in a *régime* of competition ?

Competition acts both as a propellor and a regulator. Under pain of being excluded from the market, it compels those under its sway to adopt the most efficacious methods, the most perfect machinery, to reduce their prices, to improve the quality of their products or services ; and we owe it to this energetic stimulant that the countries in which industrial and commercial liberty are most complete surpass all others in activity and riches. At the same time, competition acts as the regulator of production and profits by lowering the repayment or profit relatively to the degree of supply ; it checks capital and labour from betaking themselves to branches of industry already sufficiently provided for ; it excites them, on the other hand, to flow into branches where they are scarce, by offering them the inducement of a profit proportioned to that scarcity. Lastly, competition creates an irresistible tendency to the universal equalisation of salaries to the margin of their necessary rate.

The most elevated branches of human activity, religious teaching, letters, fine arts, etc., are ruled by this natural law every whit as much as the lower

branches of material production.   The salutary effects
upon the zeal and conduct of the ministers of worship
of religious competition are, in all times and places, as
certain as are the sloth and corruption which monopoly
inevitably produces.   These facts were so manifest
that even in times when religion found itself united
to the State and rigorously protected against all
other rivalry, the Church appreciated the necessity of
lessening or correcting the vices of the monopoly by
multiplying the religious orders who worked in competition with the secular clergy, and thus a struggle
came into existence, which at times—when both appealed to identical classes of the population—acquired
an extraordinary acerbity.

We can also ascertain, although this seems less
apparent, the regulative effects of competition upon
the property and revenue of religious bodies.   These
effects, we say, are less obvious, since, save in the
United States, the principle is vitiated by privileges
or subsidies accorded to certain bodies.   In England,
for example, where the Church has preserved the monstrous privilege of imposing the tithe on the members
of dissenting sects, the Church enjoys a revenue out
of all proportion to the necessary retribution of her
services.[1]   But even in this very case, the regulative

[1] [This is hardly accurate.   The fact that the endowments of
the Church are annually augmented by voluntary contributions
exceeding the enormous amount of £5,000,000 is clear proof that
the Church is none too rich when the vast scope of its work is
considered. .The poverty of rural benefices is a fact of terrible
significance.   What is required is *redistribution*. Bishop Stere
once said that England requires a cheap clergy.   This may represent the spiritual necessities of the case, but it must be re-

action of competition makes itself felt. The sacrifices the English people have imposed on themselves, in the Church's favour, the riches which it has showered upon it, the tithe which it has consented to pay, have acted as an impulse to encourage the multiplication of rival sects. In proportion to the numerical and moral increase of these sects they have swept away a portion of the increasing revenues of the Established Church, and when at last she is deprived of her privileged position—and this will be ere long—the flagrant and wicked inequality of her position relatively to rivals will little by little disappear. We may safely prophecy that the very excess of her resources, so far from assisting her in her struggle for existence, rather acts as a cause of her decline. It is the same thing as we see in industry; the old houses, basing themselves on the importance of their capital, the extent of their credit and reputation, allow themselves to relax their activity, to decline little by little and give place to younger rivals, less rich indeed, but stirred up by the very inferiority of their position to raise themselves higher; while this necessary energy is lacking to those who have already arrived at the pinnacle.

Property and liberty are, therefore, the requisites of religious just as much as of industrial progress. The right of acquiring and preserving movable and

membered that the English clergy are, rightly or wrongly, required to maintain a certain social position. A cheap clergy would be a celibate clergy. Protestant liberationists who look to disestablishment and disendowment as a cure for Anglican sacerdotalism must look this prospect in the face.]

immovable capital, and of disposing of it without let
or hindrance, procures for the clergy security and
independence together with the means of improving
and extending their operations. The liberty of choosing
between the different systems gives rise to competition
and causes a double progress ; a constant and mutual
emulation of activity and an approximation as complete as possible of their work to the level of intellectual development possessed by their supporters. This
approximation is the first and most indispensable condition of progress and fruitfulness in religious culture ;
since a religion whose ideas and practices are below or
above the intellectual and moral capacity of those to
whom it is addressed is bound to have no hold upon
them, and failing to furnish them with digestible
food, it can neither maintain nor develop the moral
force whose religious feeling—the love or fear of a
god or of a spirit—brings to the service of individual
self-restraint and the government of society.

This moral force, which man derives from religion,
which has accumulated in him and his progeny,
which becomes exhausted and dies out when it is not
fed, is no less necessary to-day than it has been in the
past.

CHAPTER XX.

LIKE all other constituent feelings of the moral side of human nature, religious feeling is universal, but unequally distributed. So long as it has only a rudimentary existence, so long is its development one-sided and almost harmful. Its insufficiency produces atheism ; its excess, mysticism. Like all other feelings, also, the feeling manifests itself in the shape of a need, and this need demands a satisfaction proper to its nature.

Religious feeling resolves itself into the love and fear of one or several beings superior in power to man. Everything tends to show that the conception of these superhuman beings is begotten by the action of natural phenomena. A special faculty in man's intelligence, his consciousness of causality (*la causalité*), compelled him to search for the authors of those external phenomena, which he is powerless to produce, and which produce in him sensations of pleasure or of pain. Who, he asked, were these agents but the powers which hold men in their power, and whom the elements obey ? These powers, as the phenomena produced by them caused man pleasure or pain, became the object of his love or

147

fear. He loved or dreaded them just as a frail being loves or dreads one superior to him in force or intelligence. Thus he could not conceive them as otherwise than endowed with appetites, passions, motives akin to his own peculiar nature. He expressed his love or fear, and he strove to obtain their benevolence or to disarm their ill-feelings, by acts whose use he had acquired in his dealings with his fellows ; to them he addressed his prayers, rendered his homage, and offered his presents. He submitted himself to their will, and obeyed their laws. His conception of these spirits or deities was in accordance with his own character and the state of development of his moral and intellectual faculties. The worship which he offered was in harmony with this conception. Hence, the diversity and inequality of religions. Yet all religions, including even the most rude, have something divine in them, since in each is preserved an aspiration directed to a being superior to a man, i.e. a god. They pass from age to age, perfecting themselves, and end by finding their most perfect expression in Christianity.

From the study of man's faculties, all of which answer to a real object and have a useful end, and from the recognition of the civilising influence of religion, it follows that the existence of the religious feeling involves that of the Deity. It is through this feeling that the human species has been able to raise itself above the other animals; it has been, so to speak, the civilising faculty of humanity. If it did not effect the formation of the first societies, it has been the instrument of their preservation and progress.

In those early days, when the powerful and elaborate mechanism which places all the forces of the nation at the disposal of the governing body had as yet no existence, how would the nascent societies have been able to exist if religious feeling had not brought to their political, moral, and economic laws, and even to their sanitary laws, the binding force of the penalties and rewards of a superhuman power? Religion has been the instrument of the creation of order. It has assured the exercise of those rights and the fulfilment of those duties which observation and experience compelled the intelligent few to recognise as necessary to the preservation and progress of society—things which demand a power of discipline and self-sacrifice beyond the capacity of the ignorant and bestial masses. This result, which governments, despite their enormous material powers, have with difficulty acquired not even in our own times, religion obtained even at the beginning of society. By means of a purely moral force, it maintained internal order at an epoch when the whole material force was required for assurance of security from without. To this social service it added the no less beneficent one which it offered to individuals, consoling them in the miseries of their present condition by the hope of a brighter future.

Have, then, these services which religion has rendered humanity ceased to be necessary? Does not the very power of civilisation suffice to justify the existence of the intelligent and beneficent power, which in the past has served to gradually elevate humanity to its actual condition? Is it true that re-

L

ligion has to-day no longer any useful *rôle* to fulfil, that
civilised societies may henceforth free themselves from
this instrument of their conservation and progress,
that the modern man has no longer any need of the
hopes and consolations which their forefathers borrowed from faith of religion ?

Without seeking to discover what may be the future
condition of societies and individuals, we may settle
this question by considering their present condition.
The progress which, on the one hand, has transformed
the machinery of production, and on the other, has
effected the emancipation of the masses by replacing
compulsory tutelage of slavery and serfdom by self-
government, has provoked the crisis, in which we are
nowadays playing our part. How may this crisis,
daily becoming larger and more aggravated, be
brought to an end ?

How will order now menaced by the cataclysm of a
social revolution be preserved ? Will the material
force concentrated in the hands of the State suffice to
safeguard it?

Beyond all doubt, the modern State has at disposal
a formidable power, but this power is hazardous, and
may be often upset by a mere breath. Should a government have no other force than the support it draws from
the nation, then the day public opinion abandons it, it
succumbs to the slightest shock. Governments the
most solid in appearance have not resisted political revolutions; will they be better able to resist social
revolutions ? But have social revolutions in their
turn any better secret than political revolutions of
putting an end to the crisis ? Will they be better

able to dispossess the middle classes (*tiers état*) in the interests of the workers (*quatrième état*)? Will they be able to put into the hands of the working classes the land, factories, machinery and raw materials? Will they put them into possession of the art of turning these things into profitable use, of re-constructing and increasing them by the useful employment of their products? Will they have the virtue of ameliorating individual "self-government," of curing sloth, incontinence, intemperance, and all other vices productive of misery and disorder? No; less even than political revolutions, social revolutions will fail to remedy the crisis: on the contrary, they will aggravate it by ruining or squandering the capital of civilisation.

This crisis, one of the gravest that humanity has passed through, can only be closed by such a progress as will at one and the same time ameliorate the government of society and "self-government." This progress, then, has as its necessary agents science which enlightens the conscience by compelling it to recognise rules useful for the government both of itself and of others, and religion, which supplies the moral force indispensable for the application and execution of these rules.

But even suppose that civilised societies are in the future able to free themselves of the assistance furnished by religion in maintaining order in their midst, and in accomplishing the reforms necessary to assure its continuance, will religion have no longer any part to play, any mission to accomplish? May we hope that there will be in the future no creatures disfavoured by nature, mal-

REESE LIBRARY
OF THE
UNIVERSITY
OF
CALIFORNIA.

treated by fortune, weak and miserable creatures, who experience the desire of being consoled for the evils of the present life by the hope of the life that is to be? Can we desire that our hearts should be hardened so as to witness unmoved the annihilation of those beings in whom our affection is centred, and not revolt against the thought that the bonds so strong, which have linked us to those dearest to us, should be broken for ever? Let us even suppose that this world, from being a vale of tears, should become an Eden, would man be better disposed to content himself with earthly happiness? Because life will be brighter, will he more easily console himself for its loss? Because science will have extended for man the limits of the universe, because it will have shown him a limitless beyond, because it will have made him contemplate the existence of habitations superior in grandeur and beauty to his own, will he resign himself better to the mediocrity of a lot cast in time and space? In culling the fruit of the tree of knowledge, did not the first man, as says the legend of the earthly paradise, condemn his descendants to hope for the joys that will ever remain for them the most deceptive of illusions? Is the always limited happiness which science is able to procure for human creatures in their transitory life sufficient to compensate for the bitterness of deprivation of those unending good things which it presents without giving any hope of possession? This hope, without which science can but be the purveyor of pessimism, belongs to religion alone to confer.

The rôle of religion is, then, not ended, and, to trust

all appearances, will not be less considerable in the future than it has been in the past. But this rôle cannot be performed with all necessary efficacy, save under conditions that procure for religion independence with liberty.

The necessary condition of religious progress is the separation of Church and State, effected not in hostility to, but in favour of religion.

PART II.

THE FUTURE OF RELIGION.

CHAPTER I.

THE conditions of religion in France, and, with certain points of difference, in the greater number of civilised states,[1] may be defined in a few words. The State recognises and guarantees the liberty of religious bodies, and it subsidises some, imposing on all certain restrictions and liabilities. It salaries the officers of recognised systems, and provides, in a certain measure, for the maintenance and increase of their propaganda, while, at the same time, it reserves to itself a control over the appointment of ecclesiastical dignitaries. It controls the relations between the Roman Catholic clergy and their chief; it limits the right of assembly, property, and propaganda of the secular and regular clergy; it imposes restrictive conditions on instruction; it exacts the service of the Church at certain ceremonies, etc. etc. The aim which the founder of this state of things, the author of the *Concordat*, sought, was the transformation of religious bodies

[1] [For the American System, *Cf.* Auguste Carlier. *La Republique Américaine*, vol. iii., p. 503.]

into a branch of the administration, and their clerical members, henceforth salaried, into officials. He did not trouble himself with the aspirations to which religion ministers, or the manner in which the system he was establishing would affect the practice of religion. He had no other interest at stake than that of his own ascendency, which he conceived in the most selfish and narrow fashion. He considered the clergy as a sort of moral police designed to secure the submission of his subjects, and more especially their acquiescence in military conscription. He even went to the excess of demanding the bishops to make themselves auxiliaries of his political police by denouncing the conspiracies woven against his government. We can but be surprised that the Catholic Church, once almost omnipotent, should resign itself to accept conditions so hard and humiliating, but she had passed through the pains of revolution, her goods had been confiscated, and she could but fear that the indifference, even hostility, of a part of her ancient supporters would leave her without resources. On the other hand, by obtaining a place in the budget, and securing thereby her material existence, she could, little by little, regain at least the position she had held before the revolutionary outburst. She knew that governments would go by while she remained, and that a new political upheaval would, in all probability, enable her to regain this regretted position. Her foresight and hope was justified by the fall of the Empire, and the advent of the Restoration. During the fifteen years' Bourbon rule, the Catholic clergy directed all their energies

towards a single end — the re - establishment of
their privileges and secular preponderance. The opposition aroused by these attempts, however, only
served to prove their impossibility. Not only did the
clergy fail in regaining their monopoly, but they
stirred up opinion against a government suspected of
partiality to schemes so retrograde. History will,
therefore, attach to the clergy no small responsibility
for the Revolution of July, 1830.

The Governments which have succeeded each other
in France since the last mentioned event have all
sprung from the Revolution. We understand, then,
why the Catholic clergy should preserve towards
them an attitude of consistent ill-feeling, and why
they have on so many occasions manifested a prefer-
ence for the heirs of the ancient monarchy. We also
understand why the Governments, on their side, have
rendered ill-will for ill-will, hostility for hostility,
and why they have studied to fetter the liberty of a
power more disposed to injure than to serve them
Since, however, either the intelligent _élite_ of the
clergy have ceased to hope for the re-establishment of
the ancient monarchy, or else have seen that a
monarchical restoration would be altogether incapable
of affording the Catholic system its former privileged
position, the power directing the Church seems at this
moment disposed to accommodate itself to the sway of
the Republic. But its advances are received with a
reserve far from encouraging, and the reconciliation
of Church and State still seems a doubtful conting-
ency, to say the least. Such is the position of affairs
to-day.

One thing, the principal point in this account of the relations of Church and State, is that these two powers, by remaining associated, after having been united by mutually specifying the conditions of their association, have never had in view more than their own interest well or badly conceived. What did the State desire by re-establishing, as far as it was possible to re-establish, the union the Revolution dissolved ? It desired to have at its disposal the influence of the Church. What did the Church desire in accepting the *Concordat*, despite the restrictions that act placed on its liberty ? She wished to have at her disposal the material resources and power of the State. Neither one nor the other of these two powers troubled itself to know which of the two systems, that of union or that of separation, was more favourable to the purposes of religion; neither one nor the other considered the general and superior interest, which economists name the "interest of the consumer." Even at the present day, this is still the case, and this is why the maintenance of the union is regarded as indispensable, as much by the politicians, who in this affair consider only the interest of the State, as by the doctors and dignitaries of the clergy, who regard only the interest of the Church. By analysing this state of opinion, we are able to account for the obstacles opposed to the separation of Church and State in France. This separation the two allies resist equally, although their motives are different, and even opposed.

The paramount idea of any political party, finding itself in office, is to turn the spiritual influence of the

Church to its purposes, or, at least, to prevent the Church from using her influence against it. The idea is to extend the ascendancy of the party, and to make it more fruitful, by subjecting to it the greatest possible number of different interests. Such an ideal would be a "national religion," a religion which would be kept in dependence, and whose influence would be at the entire disposal of the predominant political party.[1] This ideal is, moreover, in perfect accord with the doctrine of State-Socialism actually in vogue, a doctrine which answers to the natural aspirations of the political and administrative world, that is, of the increasingly numerous and influential class who live by the fulfilment of State services. Supposing that this doctrine came to be applied in its fulness, all the departments of human activity, those which minister to intellectual and moral wants as well as those which afford satisfaction for material ones, would be absorbed by the State, and engulfed in the domain of public administration. And notice that State-Socialism is at the present day almost universally regarded as the ideal to which our civilised societies ought to tend! The only difference we are able to distinguish between the radical or revolutionary and the conservative Socialists, is that the former wish to realise this ideal immediately, by brushing aside all resistance, and by confiscating without compensation all the property and industries which it will unite with the domain of the State ; while the con-

---

[1] [Cardinal Newman has somewhere said that Liberals love a "tame Church"—a sort of jackdaw to dance about their lawn with clipped wings.]

servative Socialists, on the other hand, wish to arrive
at this end by degrees, by indemnifying private interests, and respecting acquired rights and even still
existing privileges. But the destination of these two
schemes is the same, if the roads leading thither
are different. The separation of Church and State is,
then, in opposition both to the things which Governments have at all times considered to be their interest,
and which the majority of persons at the present day
still regard as progress. It is not less contrary to the
things which the clergy, from the point of view of
the "producer," also regard as their own interest,
nay, even as the ideal in matters of religion. Whatever
may be the nature of the production, whether its
scope be material, intellectual or moral, whether it be
agriculture, industry, art, instruction or worship, nearly
every producer, with the exception, perhaps, of a very
few, is a partisan of monopoly ; all aspire to the possession of a market from which competition will be excluded. In their eyes, competition is the enemy, and
when they despair of suppressing it, they at least set
themselves to limiting it, for competition compels
each individual to make severe efforts and heavy sacrifices, and destroys without pity the hindmost. Monopoly is, on the other hand, rest, peaceable possession,
the greatest profit in return for the least expenditure.

This purely worldly view must be balanced by one
of a more elevated character, *viz.* that every religion
considers itself to be in sole possession of the truth.
The Catholic Church, in particular, affirms that all
other religions are the work of the devil, and that

they lead their followers to eternal damnation.[1] Thus the Catholic clergy thought it their duty not only to persuade the infidels or schismatics to abandon their false religion for the true, but in case of their refusal, to compel them to do so. In order to be able to do this, the clergy employed force, and consequently had recourse to the secular arm for the coercive jurisdiction belonging to the State. The Catholic Church might well have been able to tolerate the co-existence and rivalry of the other systems had she not possessed the power necessary for their suppression or expulsion, but this power she devoted herself to acquire, and, when lost, she sought to recover it. Her ideal is that the Church should be mistress of the State, that the State should, as an obedient and docile agent, secure, by force or persuasion, the rule of the true faith. The separation of

[1] [M. Molinari uses the term Catholic (in continental sense of the term) to express the portion of the Church which regards communion with the see of Rome as essential to salvation. We suppose that no instructed Romanist would find any objection with the following statement of Dr. Pusey : "They are members of the soul of the Church, who not being members of the visible communion and society, know not that in not becoming members of it, they are rejecting the command of Christ, to whom in faith and love and in obedience they cleave. And they being members of the *body* or visible communion of the Church, are not members of the *soul* of the Church, who, amid outward profession of the faith, do in heart or deeds deny them whom in words they confess. The deliverance promised in that day, is to those who being in the body of the Church, shall by true faith in Christ, and fervent love to Him, belong to the soul of the Church also, and who, though not in the body of the Church, shall not *through their own fault* have ceased to be in the body, and shall belong to its soul, in that through faith and love they cleave to Christ its head."]   II.

Church and State is, then, in manifest opposition to an essential point in the Roman propaganda, and this fact explains why a pope so enlightened and liberal as Leo XIII. refuses to accept such a solution.

But even were the Catholic Church able to admit the principle of separation, she has under existing circumstances a serious cause for rejecting it. By whom has this question been placed in 'the order of the day' but by a mere fraction of the Radical and Socialist party? Has it been anything more than a piece of electoral warfare against clericalism? The theory is, as we have remarked, in complete accordance with the design the Radicals and Socialists pursue— the completest possible absorption of private activities by the State. The separation is only demanded by an insignificant group of fanatical atheists, who consider religious feeling a malady of humanity's infancy, and religions as the superstitions, which, begotten of ignorance and fear, priests and rulers have employed in order to subjugate and exploit the people. According to the democrat, science has meted out justice to these superstitions, for whose disappearance, which will be to the great advantage of human progress, it will suffice on one side to extend education amongst the masses, and, on the other, to deprive all religions of State subsidies, and to check their capacities by sup- pressing their rights of property and association, and to regain what they have usurped. Such is the aim of the majority of sincere promoters of the separa- tion. We can see why religious souls, not to mention the Church herself, cannot but refuse to accept it.

Taking these circumstances into consideration, we

are tempted to believe in the impossibility of a separation which seems equally repugnant to either set of allies, a measure which, at the present moment, is only contended for by an insignificant number of Radicals and Socialists, hostile to all religion, a measure in contradiction to the general tendency of the doctrines of even these last. Yet the separation will come about, since it is necessary.

There is, however, an interest, without which, since it must become absolutely paramount, both Church and State will have to reckon—the interest of the masses who form the *clientèle* of either These masses have need of religious education, and the inadequacy of that moral instruction causes an injury no less severe than that which would be effected by the loss of those branches of production which satisfy material wants. History attests the fact that the cultivation of religious feeling is an indispensable factor in the preservation and prosperity of nations, that each time this sentiment is weakened, the nations fall further into decadence, and their Church and State dragging them down in their fall, they end in disappearing from the scene of existence. In religious, as in all other matters, it is, therefore, the interest of the greatest number which ought to be regarded, for this interest contains in itself that of Church and State, and it is the system best adapted to this interest that must finally prevail.

To convince ourselves that the best system is that under which religious bodies enjoy the greatest amount of independence and liberty, it suffices to take a simple survey of the state of religious culture among the different peoples belonging to our civilisation. It is apparent that this culture is both most widely spread and most perfect in the United States and in England, where the number of religious practitioners is most considerable, and where, at the same time, religious sentiment is freed from low and rude superstitions. On the other hand, it is in the countries where religious monopoly has had the most lengthy existence, in Italy, Spain, and in those countries where it still remains, Russia, for example, that the higher classes are the least religious, and the lower devoted to the vilest superstitions, and religious feeling exercises the slightest influence over the morality of the people. If, then, morality has religious feeling as its basis, and religious feeling is necessary for the preservation and progress of nations, does not experience induce the people to adopt the condition best qualified to develop and improve the culture of religion ?

Unfortunately, nations are slow to apprehend the lessons of experience, and still slower to profit by them. This is why, to judge by appearances, so many long years will have to pass by before the general interest in religious culture, in lands where this culture has not yet ceased to be monopolised, will have at its service a well defined opinion, powerful enough to deal with interests which, selfish and blind in their egotism, throw obstacles in the way of the establishment of religious independence and liberty. But, none the less, this rule will ultimately prevail, since it is necessary, and since the nations who refuse to adopt it will fall vanquished in the inevitable universal struggle of competition.

The following quotations illustrate the attitude of the present Pope to the matters discussed in the previous chapter :—
In his encyclical of February 16th, 1892, addressed to archbishops, bishops, clergy, and all the Catholics of France, the Pope Leo XIII. has condemned the principle of separation in these terms :—" To separate Church and State is equivalent to the separation of human legislation from Christian and Divine. We are not at this moment desirous of demonstrating the theological absurdity of this separation; everyone will, without our aid, understand this. When the State refuses to render to God the things that are God's, it, by a natural consequence, refuses to render to the citizens things they have a right to as men, for, whether one likes it or not, the true rights of man spring entirely from his duties towards God. When it happens that the State in this respect, neglects the principal object of its institution, it will, in fact, end by stultifying itself, and contradicting the very reason of its natural existence. These higher truths are so clearly enunciated by the voice of natural reason that they are binding on every man who is not blinded by the violence of passion. Catholics, therefore, cannot too strongly check themselves from abetting such a separation. However, to wish that the State should separate itself from the Church is, by logical consequence, to wish that the Church should be reduced to the liberty of living under the rights common to all citizens. . It is true that this is the position in certain countries. It is a state of existence, which, if it has many and grave disadvantages, offers also certain advantages, especially when the legislator, by a fortunate inconsistency, has not ceased to avail himself of Christian principles ; and these advantages, although they neither suffice to justify the false principle of separation, nor authorise its defence, still render, worthy of toleration a state of things which, practically, is not the worst of all. But in France, a nation Catholic by its traditions and where the faith is still by the great majority of its sons, the Church ought not to be placed in the doubtful position in which it is situated amongst other peoples. Catholics will so much the less advocate separation as they become better acquainted with the intentions of the foes who desire it. As regards these last— and they speak their mind clearly—this separation is the entire independence of political and religious legislation ; nay, it is more— it is the absolute indifference of the civil power to the interests of the Christian society, that is to say the Church, and, moreover the negation of its existence."

[*Cf.* Hergenröther : *Catholic Church and Christian State*, English Translation, vol. i., p. 27. " The Church can often be content if her rights as a corporation are respected and protected ;.but she can never regard as a true doctrine that which disregards her divine origin and divine rights."]

CHAPTER II.

THAT morality is the indispensable vehicle of national preservation and progress, and that its invariable basis is in religious feeling, are truths that cannot too often be insisted upon. We have attempted in a previous volume to demonstrate the economic functions of morality. In analysing the aggregate of rights and duties which constitute it, we have stated that the observation of the first and the fulfilment of the latter are needful (that is to say, they contribute to the preservation and progress of the human species), and that every infraction of right, every breach of duty, causes a loss of the vital energy upon which the duration and propagation of the species is dependent. The agreement of justice, the object of morals, with utility, the object of political economy, is sufficiently admitted, and we can consider this as a principle added to science.

But if the economic *rôle* of morality is not seriously contested, it is otherwise with the moral *rôle* of religion. Certain persons do not cease from alleging that no relation exists, that there is no necessary bond between morality and religion, that religious feeling is without influence upon morality, and that religion is, therefore, no indispensable agent of the preservation and progress of society and the species. We shall,

however, discover this relationship, the link binding
morality to religion, if we analyse the effects of the two
beliefs which engender the religious sentiment—the belief in the existence of God, that is to say, of a Being
infinitely superior to man in power and moral beauty,
and in the immortality of the soul—beliefs that cannot be separated.[1]

Man, like all other creatures, obeys motives of pain
and pleasure. This is an instinctive and blind motive
which only too often drives man to injure himself and his
brethren. What then can avail to master and regulate
in him the power of this instinct, save the fear of pain
and the hope of a superior pleasure ? But if we believe
that no superhuman and infallible power exists, if we
believe that the life of man is limited to this earth,
there is no certainty in justice. Man may with impunity infringe it, set the moral law at defiance, and
damage his fellow, in order to satisfy his own appetite. In fact, society has provided for the necessity
of checking attacks on another's life and property, and
has also, by penalties more or less rigorous rendered
obligatory the fulfilment of obligations recognised as
indispensable for the security and preservation of the
race; but legal coercion is defective and uncertain. Too
many malefactors are always escaping! Too many
remain in honour and impunity! Too many of the just
remain miserable and despised after a life of privations
and suffering. But only believe, as religious feeling
irresistibly incites you to believe, in the existence of
an Infinite Power, just and good, believe that the
earthly life is not the span of personal existence, then,
and only then will you see that the penalties that

[1] See above, part i., chap. xii.

some incur, and the rewards that others merit, acquire
a character of certitude, and then and then only will
the sentiment of justice innate in the human heart
be satisfied.   On this condition only is order assured,
and morality founded on a basis that cannot be shaken.

Again, the moral influence of religious faith acts in
yet another way.   If man believes in the existence of
an infinitely powerful Being who is just and good, he
will be irresistibly drawn towards Him, he will devote
himself to imitating Him and pleasing Him by submission to the rules of conduct which He has laid down
for the good of His creatures, and he will pray for
succour to surmount the temptations that beset his
observance of these rules.   If he is convinced that the
earthly life is but a short preparation for the eternal,
the transitory joys and sufferings of this present life
will seem, the former less desirable, the latter more bear-
able ; he will be less ardent in the search for pleasure,
and if he can only obtain pleasure by the infraction of
the moral law, he will be restrained by the twofold
fear of offending Him who is the object of his adoration
and of incurring a lasting pain in return for a passing
pleasure ; he will suffer privations and wrongs with
resignation and patience, and as he undergoes these
in obedience to the divine law they will seem but
just.

Thus, in the same way that the observation of
moral laws is necessary to the preservation and progress of the human species, religious feeling appears
to be the necessary machinery for securing observance,
since it brings to the support of these laws the co-operation of an eternal hope, and thereby renders their observance more easy—more easy, because to the mono-

poly of pleasure and pain which irreligion imparts to our earthly existence, religion opposes the competition of infinite joys and sufferings in eternity.

The strength of morality, however, is proportioned to its adaptability to the changing conditions of social life. In our days, the progress of the arts of destruction which has permanently secured the supremacy of the civilised world and placed it beyond the attacks of barbarians, and the progress of the arts of production which has developed economic relations between peoples and individuals, have necessitated a corresponding progress in the application, if not the principles of morals.[1] Law, after being useful, and therefore moral, has often become injurious, and therefore immoral. The development of exchange in time and extent has given rise to a multitude of circumstances which hitherto only existed in germ; the distribution of products between the factors of production, for instance, has become a most complicated and difficult problem to solve. This distribution is effected through the agency of the economic laws controlling production and exchange; but the operation of these laws must not be fatalistic, but regulated by human will; the distribution may well be of more or less utility, and therefore of proportionate morality. How ought these laws to work for general utility and justice, for the highest economic and moral end? These questions and many others demand an evolution and progressive extension of morals; at the same time, the emancipation of subject classes who have now become free and responsible for their destiny, has universalised the necessity for the knowledge of rights and duties,

[1] See Molinari: *La Morale Economique*, bk. v., chap. vii.

and the necessity of an increase in moral forces requisite for the profitable government of self. Under the former state of subjection, the multitude had no desire to govern itself; it was governed; it was content to obey blindly the laws and rules imposed on it, and if the moral force to conform was lacking, its governors and masters employed brute force to compel obedience. The knowledge of rights and duties and the moral force which exacted the observance of the one and the performance of the other, was felt unnecessary so long as the minority ruled; these things were of no use to the governed majority. To-day they are indispensable to the free and responsible members of civilised society.

But evolution and the expansion of morality is clearly out of pace with the progress which has so profoundly and rapidly changed the conditions of social life. Of the laws regulating social and individual conduct, a good number have lost all *raison d'etre*, and have, after being the instruments of preservation and progress, become causes of weakness and decadence. On the other hand, the masses, now charged with the free execution of rights and duties, are but ill-taught to recognise them, and they have not as yet acquired sufficient moral force to render self-constraint certain. Hence the reappearance of the disorders and evils which afflict our modern society and even overbalance the acquisitions of material progress, turning its use to evil ends. Hence, also, the severe crisis through which we are now passing.

It is, as we have said, the province of science, now separated from religion, to observe the evils caused by the lack of adaptation of moral laws to the actual

circumstances of social existence and to secure their
adaptation ; in a word, it belongs to science to fulfil
the labour of observation, experimentation, and invention necessary for the progress of the moral rules
relative to the government of self and others. It also
belongs to science to popularise these rules, to demonstrate how their observation is dictated by the general
and permanent interests of humanity, to show that
the respect for every right and the performance of
every duty produces a grand total of utility, that
every infraction of right, every breach of duty, causes
a positive evil, that the utility or evil effected in the interest of the whole re-acts on the individual, whence it
follows, in the first place, that the moral or immoral
conduct of each individual has its influence for good
or evil on the general lot, and in the second, that each
in contributing to create the greatest sum of utility
by the strict observation of moral laws, offers to the
total a contribution which may so come back to him, so
that the most extended interest of the individual consists in conforming himself to those laws, and thereby
bringing himself in accord with the interest of the
greatest numbers.   Such is the conclusion, and such
is the lesson of " Economic Morals."

But will this conclusion and this lesson, based
surely as they so are on observation and experience
suffice to make the individual act in a manner conformable to the general interest ? The re-action of
the general interest upon the particular is far off and
uncertain, while the enjoyment caused by an infraction of moral laws is perhaps immediate and certain.
Again, the share that the general good yields the
individual may be beneath his desires. If the occa-

sion should present itself to obtain with but slight, if
with any, risk at all, a larger share at the cost of the
others, why should he abstain ?   He is incited by
motives of pleasure and pain like all other creatures !
What restraint will be sufficiently strong to hold him
back ?

Such a restraint religion alone possesses, since it
alone can procure for those who obey the moral law
an enjoyment superior to all other enjoyments, and to
inflict on infringers a pain worse than all pains—
either alternative being assured and inevitable.
Economic morality has but an inadequate, uncertain
sanction ; religious morality has a sanction invariably
efficacious and certain.

But religion not only brings to morality its needful
sanction, but forges and supplies its very machinery—
the moral sense and the force which it opposes to the
appetites actually inciting man to wrong others
and self.   We are acquainted with the primary
processes in the formation of moral laws. . . . .
The moral sense sprang from religious feeling.   This sense developed itself, like all others,
by practice, and strengthened itself by the custom of
obedience to the laws.   In so developing itself, it became detached from religious feeling, and so autony-
mous.   Yet despite this separation, the moral sense in
no less a degree derives from religion the force that feeds
it and causes its victory over contrary impulse in the
government of self and others.   However highly developed, it is, while unaided, powerless to always resist
the assault of appetites seeking lawless satisfaction.
Each time it is conquered in the struggle it decreases,
and at length will end in a total loss of energy.   If, how-

ever, it is based on the eternal hopes and dread of religious faith, the combined resistance will prove triumphant. This is why it has been said that in all times and in all places the observation of moral law will be in strict relation to the growth of religious feeling. When the latter is weakened or corrupted, morality decreases, public and personal government become less moral, and, therefore, less profitable; the increase in the means of production effect an inadequate remedy for the vicious employment of wealth; injurious expenses, public and private, increase, and society falls into decline.

This weakening of morality is at the present day only too evident. It is particularly manifest in countries where religious culture is placed under the rule of strict monopoly and control, since the condition of improvement and extension in this culture do not differ from those of any other branch of human activity. Property and liberty are, in short, as necessary for religious establishments as they are for industrial. But we must bear in mind that in matters of religion, as in matters of industry, public opinion remains generally in favour of " protection." In France, for instance, one no more dreams that religion can subsist without a minister of public worship than the production of materials of life can be carried on without a minister of agriculture, of industry, and of commerce. It will be only when the evils of the actual state of religious protectionism shall have so accumulated as to become unsupportable, that opinion, at last converted by experience, will set to work to emancipate religious culture from the bonds of a superannuated régime.

CHAPTER III.

CONSEQUENCES OF THE ESTABLISHMENT OF ECONOMIC LIBERTY IN RELIGIOUS BODIES.

THE economic liberty of religious bodies meets in France with two kinds of adversaries, the Radicals and the Conservatives. The former desire to suppress the State-aid of the sects, although still preserving and aggravating the restriction of their rights of property, freedom of association, education, and preaching, etc. The end they have in view is the extinction of religion, which they consider to be a superstition incompatible with progress. From fear, however, of arousing the opposition of religious persons, they check themselves from avowing this design. They state as a reason for restricting religious liberty the danger in which this liberty would undoubtedly involve society if the power and wealth of a clergy, so powerful as the Catholic, were allowed to increase. Freedom of endowment and association would enable the clergy, so they say, to acquire little by little private property and pass it into *mortmain*, while unrestricted liberty of teaching would mould the rising generations to their will, and so civilisation would soon be submerged in a sort of mediæval darkness.

176

If the Catholic clergy were still in possession of the religious monopoly and privileges of taxation and education which they once enjoyed, then these fears would have some foundation, although experience has shown that neither the excess of their riches nor their exclusive hold on the education of the young has really served such a purpose. But would a clergy, compelled to depend solely upon the free contributions of their flock for the costly maintenance of living, for the material means to build and keep in good repair churches, presbyteries, convents and schools, and for the provision for the expenses of ceremonial, etc., and all this in face of the free and unlimited competition of rivals—would such a clergy be able to become wealthy with ease? And if indeed this were ever to happen, would there fail to re-appear the abuses inherent in excess of wealth, corruption, favour-itism, routine, relaxation of activity and zeal, the very things which under the ancient *régime* ended in the alienation of esteem and the revolutionary out-burst? And, under the competitive state, the chastise-ment would be more prompt and less detrimental to the general interests of society. To the extent an avaricious priesthood neglects the performance of its spiritual duties in order to give itself up to covetousness of temporal goods, the easier are its rivals able to win over the hearts of the religious, and supersede the clergy whose revenues they will appropriate. If this same clergy, animated by a foolish hatred of civilisation, at-tempts to extinguish the love of civilisation in the ris-ing generation by hiding from them the discoveries of science, will not the inferiority of their teaching lead to

REESE LIBRARY
OF THE
UNIVERSITY
OF
CALIFORNIA.

the desertion of their schools and universities for those of their rivals ? The real or pretended apprehensions which the economic liberty of religious bodies inspires in Radicals have no basis in fact. The re-establishment of priestcraft, the absorption of property in *mortmain,* the systematic degradation of the young, etc. etc., are to-day mere political catch-words.

In fear lest the suppression of State support should deprive the Catholic Church of its necessary means of subsistence, the Conservatives are hostile to economic liberty, hoping to maintain in France the system of the *Concordat,* with the exception, perhaps, of certain conditions. In localities where the population is numerous and well-to-do, voluntary contributions, together with the revenues of clerical property, might possibly suffice ; but this, they say, is not the case in poor parishes. In default of the resources necessary to support her work, the Church will, it is contended, be obliged to abandon by no means the least important part of her charge. All we can say is, that the Conservatives who plead this objection and entertain such a fear, do not appreciate the real position of religious bodies in a state of full liberty. A Church is nothing else than a religious State. The religious State ought, like a political State or a commercial body, to constitute and organise itself in the way best suited to its object. Supposing that liberty became established and universalised, the religions or sects would form so many " States," each having its Government, administration, and budget, divided and sub-divided like a political State into more or less numerous districts. In such a way as

experience proves necessary, the religious States will
be more or less centralised. Taking into account the
vastness of her domain, which extends over different
parts of the globe, and comprises not less than 250
millions of faithful—that is a population more
numerous than any political State, China and Eng-'
land excepted—the Roman Catholic Church must con-
tinue to be governed by her own sovereign authority
and a decentralised administration, each province,
each diocese, each parish having its own special administration and finance. But this decentralisation
ought not to exclude the hierarchical subordination of
the parts to the whole, and the application of a portion of local resources to general requirements. Under
a state of competition which will oblige each Church
to adopt an organisation at once the most effective
and economic, this subordination and share of revenues
will be established in such a way as experience will
prove most useful. In a great religious State, such
as the Roman Catholic, the general resources will
naturally amount to a considerable sum, however
small may be the percentage of contributions of individual parishes. These percentages will suffice to cover
deficits in the balance-sheets of localities too poor to
pay for their own religious requirements, or to provide
for such other purposes as the Church may judge to be
for the good of religion. We need, then, have no fear
that the insufficiency of means in any particular locality
will compel the Church to leave any portion of the soil
uncultivated. The Church will have a double interest
in supplying means out of its general resources : a re-

ligious interest in the salvation of souls, a mundane interest in the preservation of its *clientèle*.

But would these local and general revenues prove superior to all demands made upon them? To this apprehension of the Conservatives, we need only oppose the fears of the Radicals, who are in terror lest lay property may be absorbed by ecclesiastical *mortmain*. We believe, however, that neither of these fears are well founded. If the resources of the Catholic Church should come to surpass its needs, this very excess will act as a cause of decadence even more readily under a system of economic liberty than under one of monopoly and privilege. We have good reason to trust that these resources will not be lacking under the new state of things, in which unfettered disposition of property, and free choice of fit persons, together with the pressure of competition, ought rather to render activity more fruitful.

Under the present system the Church is subsidised, but places of worship have, for the most part, ceased to belong to her;[1] her possession is precarious, and she is bound to address her claims for her necessary maintenance, and for assistance in artistically decorating her sanctuaries, to a Government usually indifferent to religious affairs. The municipalities and governments lack competence in matters of sacred art, and they are guided in their choice of artists by considerations which have nothing in common with those of religion. They have, moreover, to provide for other things which they consider to be even more

[1] [It is hardly necessary to point the vast difference between the French and English systems].

important, and only devote to religious architecture and painting the scrapings of their budget. Need we, then, be astonished, if these arts have fallen into decay, since they have lost a patronage able to appreciate them and sufficiently rich to undertake their cost? How could religious art fail to be deserted for more lucrative, but yet inferior, branches of art? Let the Church return to her own, then she will provide as of old the just payment for the works of the great masters; religious art will be born again, and regain the foremost place, and contribute anew to the uplifting of souls to the divine ideal.

It is natural that the governments, while supplying the Church with a portion of her necessary resources, should wish to interfere in employment, and that they should seek rather their own interests than those of religion. It is for this reason we see the Italian governments striving with the French in generously subsidising the churches and religious orders in Asia, although in so doing they reduce the proper subsidies at home. The end they have in view is certainly not the propagation of the Catholic faith; they merely aim at increasing the political influence of Italy at the expense of that of France. In the eyes of politicians, be they Italian, French, or any one else, the business of priests and missionaries is before all a political business, and they pay their subsidies only as this business is performed. The Asiatic governments, however, upon whom European statesmen impose under penalty of usurious indemnities, the obligation of paying for these particular missionaries — the Asiatic governments, we say, indeed the peoples themselves, only regard the missionaries with perfectly justifiable feelings of dislike and hostility—feelings which react upon religion itself. Conversions are rare and are not worth their cost. Would they not be more numerous and of better quality if the missionaries, instead of appearing as political agents, devoted themselves entirely to the spread of the faith?

To the advantages accruing from the free employment of the Church's resources, the separation will add those accruing from the free choice for the ministry and the Church's freedom of self-government. The subsidised bodies are only able to recruit their ministry from the ranks of the nation, to establish their districts and hierarchy within the frontiers of the country; the heads of the hierarchy are nominated by the government, which also controls their relations with the sovereign pontiff. What can these rules and restrictions be more than so many obligations that, enslaving the practice of religion, diminish its means of action, and weaken its authority? Of course, this authority is to be feared if employed for political ends. But would an independent and free Church, a Church whose property and liberty would be placed under the guarantee of common-law, would such a Church have any interest in placing its influence at the service of any one party or other? It would matter little to it whether the form of government was republican or monarchical when it had nothing to fear from the republic, nothing to hope from the monarchy.

The day when the Catholic Church disengages itself from politics in order to devote itself exclusively to the accomplishment of its mission and to extend and

improve its divine work, will not that day witness the
increase of her influence and authority? Will not the
independence she will enjoy—an independence appertaining to the whole of Catholicism—enable her to
freely appreciate the morality of the acts of government and public opinion? Instead of sanctioning
unjust undertakings and chanting *Te Deum* in cele-
bration of victories of might over right, will she
not be able to use her authority in opposing the
excitement of a false patriotism, and, on every
occasion, placing her influence on the side of justice
and peace? Will not even the strongest and least
scrupulous of governments be compelled to reckon
with this moral power whose jurisdiction has no other
boundaries than those of Catholicism and whose
verdicts will be accepted and sanctioned by the con-
sciences of millions of faithful? And if she becomes
sufficiently independent to judge and condemn immorality, and if she also strives to protect everywhere
and always the feeble against the iniquities of the
powerful, will not she win for herself a host of
sympathisers?

But what will be the effects of this system upon
the present state and respective positions of the
different religions? Will it result in the breaking
up of the great religions into a multitude of sects, or
in engrafting different religions and sects in a single
uniform system? Each of these occurrences is
alike opposed to the nature of men and things. If,
in the United States, the springing up of sects was
the first result of liberty of worship, this movement of diffusion was followed by one of concentration

caused by a sense of the greater force of union and concord. But did this concentration end in uniformity? Did the competition of creeds end in the establishment of a vast religious monopoly? Not to mention especially the economic impossibility of the maintenance of such a monopoly, uniformity has to encounter an insurmountable obstacle in the diversity and inequality of the moral state and religious conceptions of different branches of the human race. The great religions, Christianity, Buddhism, Mahomedanism, are suited to their adherents, and for centuries they have made no appreciable encroachment on one another's domains. Religious diversity will then perpetuate itself, for it is based upon natural differences in civilisation and temperament. If the economic liberty of religious bodies does not result in breaking up existing religions, it will not on the other hand give birth to the colossal monopoly of a single religious state. Religious culture will extend and perfect itself by leaving to different branches of the great human family the institutions and practices best adapted to varying conceptions of things divine.

CHAPTER IV.

WE trust that it has been clearly shown that the economic freedom of religious bodies ought to result in the extension and improvement of religious culture. But are not current faiths bound to modify themselves? Must not new dogmas supersede the old? Must not present beliefs, like as paganism, druidism, and other imperfect conceptions have already done, give place to beliefs better adapted to our knowledge and civilisation? Are not religions, like all other manifestations of human activity, bound to submit to the laws of progress?

History proves that religion does not afford any exception to this law of change; yet religious progress has conditions of its own. In studying the past of the religions, we have seen how each faith possesses its peculiar dogmas, institutions, and legislation in harmony with the temperament and degree of civilisation extant among the people in whose midst they exist; and we have seen how certain beliefs are common to all religions. The deities to whom homage is done communicate or reveal their wishes and enunciate their laws either by intermediaries, divines, or prophets, or else by incarnating themselves in a human creature; their nature, type of worship, laws, and the

185

penalties and rewards which sanction these laws differ one from another, although numerous points of resemblance between these various conceptions can be pointed out. All religions have, however, two common characteristics: (1) belief in the existence of a Being infinitely superior to all other super-human or human beings, Who governs the world, rewarding those who obey His laws, and punishing those who infringe them; and (2) the belief in the immortality of the soul.

These two beliefs are the necessary basis of all religions, from which they are inseparable. Suppress the belief in the existence of a being superior to man, religion becomes void of meaning; suppress belief in the immortality of the soul, man will have no longer any reason for adoring an unknowable and irresponsible deity, and this will all the more be the case now that science has assigned natural causes to the benevolent or harmful occurrences which affect man's nature. In whatever respects the religions of the future may differ from those of the past, they will still be bound to rest on these two dogmas; they cannot have any other basis.

Religious progress, then, is limited by conceptions proper to every creed. The nature but not the existence of the Deity may be changed, the motives and objects of His activity, His intervention in the moral and material government, His relations with humanity, the laws He imposes, and the sanctions they necessitate, and the destinies they involve, may be altered, but not the fact of the existence of the immortal soul. Again, within these limits, progress is restricted to such parts of the heritage of religions as are accessible to human intelligence and the scope of science. For although the imagination can doubtless conceive the Deity differently than Christianity, for instance, has conceived Him, yet in history we find that when anyone has wished to render Christianity legendary, he has been unable to put anything but a sterile hypothesis in its place.[1]

Religious traditions usually possess many conceptions within the criticism of science, and these have already been modified, or in time will be. These modifications religions are bound to accept under the pain of compromising their authority, or losing their influence on men of light and leading. They may be classified under two heads: (1) those necessitated by the advance of natural and physical sciences; (2) those necessitated in the application of moral laws by the changes in the conditions of social life.

The error of religions, or to speak more correctly, of the trustees of their dogmas and traditions, is to consider as immutable the lessons which they have drawn from the science of their times, and to think that all which they have prescribed in moral and sanitary matters is still adequate to satisfy the present and diverse necessity of preservation and order. It is for this reason that they find themselves in conflict with the natural and

[1] Cf. Guizot: *Méditations sur l'Essence de la Religion Chrétienne*, p. 130. It is always necessary to remember that the borderland of the knowable and the unknowable has not been fixed. The ground still open for useful investigations and hypothesis is simply vast.

physical sciences, especially since the progress in the
methods and instruments of observation has given
an extraordinary impetus to these sciences, and since
the combined progress in the arts of production and
destruction has profoundly changed the conditions of social existence, and rendered harmful moral obligations
which were previously necessary.[1] However, in this
contest all the faults are not on one side. If religion
shows itself too obstinate in maintaining its traditions
and prescriptions, science, in its turn, shows itself too
eager to impose theories whose truth it has not as yet
verified, and practices whose morality is as yet
doubtful.

The acquisitions which science has made up to the
present day have in reality served rather than injured
religion. We may, perhaps, be permitted to believe
that this will be the case in the future.. Originally
the domain of the Deity comprised no more than a
single tribe and its territory ; later it extended itself
to the whole of humanity and the globe it occupies; to-
day it embraces an innumerable multitude of worlds,
whose composition science has analysed and proved to
be so like our own that we may conclude they serve as
the habitations for human beings like ourselves. To
avail ourselves of a favourite expression of the St.
Simonian school, the discoveries of science have resulted " *d'élargir Dieu* "—in compelling us to conceive
an incomparably higher idea of His power. But
suppose that the theory of evolution should be
clearly proved, and that other theories joined in
diminishing, in favour of natural laws, the direct

[1] See Molinari : *La Morale Economique*, bk. iv.

participation of the Deity in the production of natural phenomena, would the Deity, therefore, have nothing to do ? Would God exist as a *roi fainéant* ? At the same time that science has freed God from the trouble of hurling thunderbolts and presiding over the weather, has it not opened up a new field of infinite extent for the exercise of His power and intelligence by destroying the old ideas concerning the nature of the heavenly bodies. In the limitless universe, suns set, others rise ; systems disappear, others spring up. It is an unceas-ing work of composition and dissolution. Can we, who know by experience that even the slightest of our tasks exacts an application of our intelligence and an effort of will, believe that this vast and stu-pendous plan is realised by the blind operation of brute forces, that no will or intelligence intervenes to direct and rule it ? Of all hypotheses would not the denial of this consequence be the most unlikely, the most repugnant to reason ?

In conclusion, religious culture has progressed like all other branches of human activity. In the first era, when insufficiency of production compelled man to concentrate his activity upon the satisfaction of his material wants and the care of his defence, this culture was coarse and rudimentary. It developed and perfected itself under the influence of progress which, by giving birth to the division of labour, com-menced the work of civilisation, elevating the intel-lectual and moral level of nations, and furnishing them with the means of supporting a picked class de-voted to the satisfaction of the religious needs of society, and also to the discovery and application of the laws essential to its preservation. To fetichism and idolatry succeeded higher conceptions of the Divine Ideal. These conceptions were diversified, and unequally elevated and pure. In the same way that the Greeks excelled in the culture of the arts and left to humanity works that come nearest to the ideal of duty, the Jews appeared as the most apt at religious culture, and in their midst was born the most perfect religion, the one which responds to the Divine Ideal of the most exalted members of the human race.

This narrative of religious progress is based on the study of history, and, indeed, on the laws of the development of civilisation. It is in full agreement with the record of all other advances which have elevated man from a state akin to bestiality to the state which he has actually arrived at. At the present stage in the march of civilisation, the religions of peoples, despite their mutual inequality and diversity, rest upon two dogmas which all have in common, and which are indissolubly united—the existence of God and the immortality of the soul. Whatever modifications science may impose on their peculiar and secondary dogmas, it is upon this twofold basis that religion will rest in times yet to come.

CHAPTER V.

UTILITY OF AN ASSOCIATION FOR SECURING THE ECONOMIC LIBERTY OF RELIGIOUS BODIES.

WE are ignorant of the goal of human life. Its beginning and its end are lost in clouds which perhaps may never break. Yet when we consider man, when we study his physical, intellectual, and moral structure, when we analyse the aggregate of forces with which he is provided and the wants he experiences, we are struck by the fact that all the constituent parts of his being correspond with the necessities of individual and general existence and progress. The sentiment of sensual love and paternity secures the continuity and propagation of generations ; the intellectual faculties served by their proper organs permit man to elevate himself above the level of bestiality ; each faculty serves an end useful and adapted to the general good. The religious sentiment, the highest of human faculties, since it is that which essentially distinguishes man from the lower species, is, considered from either the individual's or the society's point of view, no exception to this rule. The religious sentiment sustains man in the hard trials of life, it consoles him for his losses, it helps him to bear up, and by hopes for the life to come it encourages him to fulfil painful duties, and to impose on himself the cruel sacrifices of our earthly life. It has been the effective instrument of the preservation, if not of the formation of primitive societies, since it is the religious sentiment that assures the observation of the laws necessary to the existence of progress, and engenders the love and respect which we classify under the term morality. If mankind had been deprived of religious sentiment, civilisation would have been impossible. Throughout the ages, despite the progress of governmental and coercive machinery, this force has remained the most efficacious instrument of civilisation and order.

As long as humanity exists, however fortunate the work of its hand, the individual will undergo inevitable suffering ; he will experience the need of succour, encouragement, and consolation. This need is satisfied by religion, for which we can see no alternative. But, is it true, as some allege, that its social work is completed ? Is it true that the governments of to-day are sufficiently powerful, that enlightenment is sufficiently spread, that the moral sense is sufficiently developed and generalised to ensure respect for rights and the fulfilment of all duties without the support of religion ? Experience does not allow us to cherish any such illusion. If the forces needed to maintain social order have increased, what is to be said of those at work to dissolve it ? If the decisive destruction of the old régime of subordination has allowed civilised peoples to realise wonderful progress in the sphere of productive arts, is it any the easier to make useful employment of wealth ? The enslaved and ignorant masses were once under control, to-day they control themselves. Obedience to the moral laws which was once forced on them, they must to-day as free-will agents force on themselves. Will their enlightenment and moral sense, even assisted by the salutary fear of the State police, ever prove sufficient? Is not religion, even more in the state of liberty than in the state of subordination, an indispensable instrument of social preservation?

If, as we think we have proved, this is the case, will it not also be obvious that the extension and improvement of religious culture is a social interest of the first order? And if, as we have also attempted to prove, monopolies, privileges, subsidies, states, and enterprises, afford an obstacle to religious as well as to all other kinds of progress, is not the enfranchisement of religion most urgent?

This necessity appears all the more obvious, when we consider the natural state of competition, or the struggle for existence which all the societies comprising humanity find to be the hard but indispensable condition of their progress. This rivalry is first manifested in war; the societies which are able to apply the totality of their forces to the contest prove the victors, and dispossess or enslave all others. But they did not owe this victory merely to the superiority of their arms or military ability. They were also dependent on the moral virtues which secure strength, courage, devotion, self-sacrifice, as well as the more obscure virtues which keep a people healthy and vigorous. To-day war has ceased to be the permanent method of the struggle for existence; but, nevertheless, this struggle has not disappeared, but

o

only transformed itself. Destructive competition has
given place to productive. The influence of industrial progress, and, in particular, of the means of
communication which have almost annihilated the
economic disadvantages, such as distance, and the
isolated and restricted markets of each nation have
made room for markets open and more and more accessible ; and in these each nation competes in agricultural,
industrial, and artistic products, whose value distributed
in profits, interests, rent, and wages constitutes the means
of existence for each member of society. In this industrial struggle, as in war, it is only the most capable
that win the victory. But, in the art of production,
just as in the art of destruction, the capacity to conquer does not only depend upon the superiority of
industrial materials and skill in putting them to use,
but also on the moral qualities of the workers. Suppose that in one of the competing nations, the moral
forces securing respect for the law and the observation of duty were debased, suppose that the governing
class only wielded its power as a means of enriching itself *per fas et nefas* at the cost of the
governed masses, suppose that in these masses the
feeling of duty was so weakened that inebriety,
debauchery, idleness levied an increasing drain on the
resources necessary for the increase of a healthy and
strong population, would not this demoralised nation
be sooner or later vanquished in the race for life ?
Would it not under the pressure of productive
rivalry, a pressure which it would be less and less
able to sustain, disappear from the scene of history,
just in the same way that under the pressure of

destructive competition the governing people of antiquity were submerged and dispossessed by lords and warriors whose vital forces had not been ruined by a corrupt civilisation ?

If then the preservation and development of moral forces are in the present and future, as they have been in the past, the necessary conditions of the prosperity and even of the existence of nations, if these moral forces can only be preserved by the succour of religion, must not the progress of religious culture, from the point of view of the interests of society, possess an importance equal if not superior to, that which by custom we attribute to the progress of society and industry ? Moreover, if the reform of the old system of religious bodies is an indispensable condition of this progress, must it not, under pain of decadence and death, be imposed on nations struggling for life ?

These things, if needs be, may be left to the working of circumstances. But the working of circumstances is indefinitely long, and strews ruin in its path. The march of progress must have its road prepared before it. The advent of a necessary reform may be hastened by proving its necessity. An association having for its object the enlightenment of public opinion, upon the nature of the obstacles thrown in the way of religious culture by state-conferred privileges and subsidies— *an Association for securing the Economic Liberty of Religious Bodies*—would perhaps be no less useful than reforming " syndicates," and we shall believe that we have lost neither time nor trouble if by writing this book we shall have given birth to the idea of founding such an association.

PRESS OPINIONS.

"Under this title, 'Religion,' M. de Molinari, the editor of the *Journal of Economists*, has just published a volume which seems to me to possess a remarkable interest in that it presents an original and substantial contribution to the defence of religious liberty. In respect to many of M. de Molinari's ideas, I should have to make some reservations, and some of an important nature; yet the leading idea of the book seems to me to be none the less just, and I have to offer the author my sincere compliments on his having stated this idea with a conciseness which places it above all further controversy. Catholics should be grateful to M. de Molinari for the excellent arguments by which he has pleaded their cause before public opinion. His book, despite a rationalistic tone disagreeable to our Christian ears, despite certain errors, is none the less the work of an honest and sincere soul, for whom principles are something more than grandiloquent words framed to please the world."—M. Yves Le Guerdec in *Le Monde*.

"The Liberalism of the author is certainly an illusion ; yet it is the illusion of a loyal and generous soul, who is indignant at the persecution practised in the name of liberty. He stigmatises the spoliation of the clergy by the despots of the Revolution, and the revolting intolerance of the factions of the day. May these noble protests in the cause of justice bring to this sincere mind the light of the faith."—E. Portalie, S.J., in *Études Religieuses Philosophiques Historiques et Littéraires* (Jesuit).

The reviewer, in the *Revue Bibliographique Universelle*, criticises M. de Molinari's argument on the ground that, as there is but one God, there can be but one truth and one religion. Hence "the Catholic clergy, without dreading competition, are able neither to provoke nor desire it, for this would be to desire the development of error." "We have thought it necessary to insist on this point since M. de Molinari's state of mind is that of many honest persons who recognise the grandeur and utility of the Catholic religion without at the same time being able to account for the fact. But whether one wishes it or not, Catholicism is a whole. Either, then, the coming age will accept it in entirety, and will thereby be enabled to witness a magnificent development of a moral and Christian democracy ; or else it will altogether reject it, and will witness civilisation sinking into immorality and anarchy."

"This book, written neither *dans notre esprit*, nor from our point of view, is interesting, since it may serve to demonstrate the necessity of faith from a social point of view."—*La Semaine Religieuse du Diocèse de Saint-Brieuc et Tréguier*.

"Unfortunately, M. de Molinari's religion does not appear to extend beyond religious feeling, and we have no more than moderate confidence in the moral force of a feeling."—*Revue Bibliographique Belge.*

"This interesting study of M. de Molinari marks an advance upon the old writings of this kind, conceived and executed without the positive limits of Christianity. There reigns here an atmosphere of sincerity, good faith, and honesty. Those who are acquainted with M. de Molinari are not surprised. Assuredly his book is by no means anti-Christian; in its tendencies and aim it is profoundly religious. The publication of such a work by one of the chiefs of the modern school of Political Economy is of no slight significance. Bastiat has died as a pious Catholic, saying as a last word to his confessor, 'In short, my reverend Father, I have always defended humanity and justice since I have taken to heart the interests of the consumer.' M. Baudrillart has recently published some fine thoughts on the Encyclical *Rerum Novarum;* and now M. de Molinari has penned a sort of preface to the 'Apology for Christianity.' It is necessary to disengage his style, arguments, and conclusions from the phraseology of the school of Smith and Say. This is an affair of style. The essence of the book is an affirmation of religious faith, of its necessity, eternity, the belief in a personal God, the efficacy of prayer, the immortality of the soul, the proclamation of the superiority of Christianity to all other religions known to history, and of its eternal youth. The defaults of M. de Molinari's book and system are obvious to the learned Christian." The review proceeds to point out the fallacy of a close analogy "between religious and industrial institutions, and that the Church cannot admit the separation of Church and State as a principle. 'Such a system may, under specific circumstances, be a positive condition of religious progress, but it is not founded upon a principle of absolute truth. Absolute religious progress will one day consist in the complete harmony of tendencies in Church and State, *distinguished* but not separated.'"—M. Felix de Breux in *Le Journal de Bruxelles.*

Notices hardly pretending to a critical nature have appeared in the *Univers* and *Revue du Monde Catholique.*

"We are late in describing a very interesting work, and one which has had a great success among the French public—we speak of M. de Molinari's new volume, entitled, 'Religion.' The author is known to everyone: he is one of our most eminent economists, and at the same time a writer of weight. This work is an essay in religious philosophy. The author examines the origin of religions, its progress and future. Unfortunately his point of view is exclusively economic, and he does not allow himself to contemplate the religious question in all its grandeur. M. de Molinari is mistaken, we think, when he makes out that the economic progress of nations has necessarily elevated their religious progress. M. Hyacinthe Layson recently spoke of this book in a letter to me, and appreciated it in a manner which appears to me perfectly just: 'M. de

Molinari has written as an economist, and only proposes to establish, by the study of facts and laws, the moral and social necessity of religion. This is a sort of religious position by no means the whole truth—yet an important truth—especially at the present day.' "—G. Volet in *Le Catholique Francaise*. (Organe de la Réforme Catholique Gallicane.)

" There are many excellent things and grave admissions in this book. M. de Molinari deals with the most important of questions, and we wish him many readers."—*Le Messenger Evangelique.*

" M. de Molinari affirms without reserve all the innate principles which are the basis of morality, and which constitute natural religion. This work is written in the seductive style, at once weighty and agreeable, natural to the author, and more especially with perfect perspicuity."—*Journal Officiél.*

" Let it be said at once that it is as an economist rather than a theologian M. de Molinari has studied the work of religions in the past and the conditions of their existence in the future. . . . Despite these reservations, this book is interesting both on account of the subject itself and the seriousness with which it is treated."— *Gazetté de France.*

" When we have commenced to vote for this separation, we shall see soon enough what its results will be."—*La Lanterne.*

" Take note that this is not an ordinary work. To contemplate religion—or rather religious questions—as one would contemplate a question of exercise or another question of Political Economy, as is done here, is surely a bold undertaking."—*Le Pays et Le Patriote.*

" The author, M. de Molinari, whose great economic and scientific labours all the world knows and appreciates, places himself outside the sects whose passions have, especially in our times, obscured and distorted this difficult problem. He dwells in the serene and impartial sphere of those high principles and historic facts which, in the march of humanity, have characterised the advance of the religious idea and social organisation. It is this that constitutes the originality of a book written not for parties, but for thinkers. . . . We will not, however, go so far as to say that we are convinced of the need of an immediate separation. In our eyes, State, Church, and Science are three grand factors which, each in its sphere, minister to public morality. These three forces are all necessary to the end of humanity. M. de Molinari himself has told us that "if science enlightens the conscience, it is religion that alone can arm it for the conflict of life." It is, then, to their association, and not their separation, we should tend."—*La Liberte.*

" M. de Molinari is placing the Christian trumpet to his lips. This is no novelty. The conservative economists, who, assailed and crippled by socialistic criticism, are resting on their last legs, ave long since committed their souls and their cause to God. M. e Molinari affects to believe that it is in good hands. In a *bizarre* work, a medley of economic theories and Cartesian crotchets, he sustains a thesis, which, to speak bluntly, is by no means original. . . . We conclude for the separation of Church and State, but for reasons opposed to these of M. Molinari. Frenchmen, in our opinion, are sufficiently intellectually emancipated to get rid of a State-subsidised cult, and to satisfy each according to his peculiar temperament, the innate need of an idea. Science, the arts, labour, the struggle to subdue the forces of nature to the wants of humanity, the social ideal, are sufficient reasons for living, for those who at least are not contented to remain tied down to their 'ego,' like Hindoos upon their navel."—E. Raiga in *La Justice*.

" As with all the works coming from the same pen, *Religion* is a book which must be read."—*Revue Britannique*.

" ' The Free Church in the Free State.' Such is the conclusion of this very remarkable book."—*Nouvelle Revue*.

" Whatever opinion may be formed of M. de Molinari's book, it will be recognised as a work of high character, which reveals in its author vast stores of knowledge and a rare power of reflection. I strongly recommend that it should be read and re-read ; the better one knows it the more one will appreciate it. To the good points which I have already freely praised, I will add another—its boldness, and this is not merely in conception and execution, but the boldness which reveals its meaning in a moment in matters where all is in confusion and conflict."—M. Gustave du Purynode in *Le Journal des Economistes*.

" In this suggestive book, of which not a line is without purpose, not a paragraph besides the point, everything is interesting. One feels that the author, who had a long task before him, has kept sowing ideas. Each of these ideas, none the less, attracts and inspires the reader. The new point of view M. de Molinari has assumed in this wide sweep of things illumines the evolution of religions, and enables us to understand their history, which is usually so complicated."—*Le Monde Économique*.

" For him religion is not only useful, but it is true. He believes in God and the immortality of the soul. I ought to add that this is the weakest part of his argument. . . . M. de Molinari, although he has been at pains to rest himself upon authorities, has not dealt with the question of the origin of religions scientifically. He has committed himself to pretended students who have formed hypothesises in regard to the origin of religion, and who have presented these hypothesis as truths, or who, having observed the superstitions of savages, black or red, have concluded that the religion of our ancestors were similar to them. M. de Molinari, like Mr. Max Müller, seems, I repeat, to ignore the Eastern philosophy of ancient religions which have been evolved from five before our epoch (Christianity, Islamism, Brahmanism, Buddhism, Taöism,

Sintöism). . . . However, such as it is, M. de Molinari's book is very useful; it presents religion as a social institution from a thoroughly true point of view."—Ch. M. Limousin in *Le Bulletin des Sommaires*.

"We are not disputing in this place the author's assertions, with which we are for the most part in perfect agreement in thought and feeling, but it concerns us to mention here the wish he expresses for a larger religious culture. The free and disinterested study of religious history is, in effect, one of the most active agents of the religious culture M. de Molinari desiderates."—*Revue de L'Histoire des Religions*.

"This book will certainly evoke a lively sensation in the world of thought and letters. Written by a layman, a student, a distinguished economist, who never abandons a most vigorous and inflexible impartiality, it must be of the greatest value.—*Journal de Pontparlier, de Montbéliard, Le Petit Comtois, de Besançon*.

"M. de Molinari is a very brilliant controversialist. He possesses a subtle pen, a right judgment, clear, original personality. His talent is limpid. He is, perhaps, too fruitful. At our point of civilisation, I am unable to see that religious lying and quackery can possess any social utility whatsoever. Let us, then, in our own time, tear up, without pity or without suffering an increase, the evil herbs from our garden."—"Philippe" in *Le Petit Lionnais*.

"There is in this book, which must be read for the sake of its style and ideas, a troubled mixture of true science and *a priori* conception of historicism and doctrinarism. If, in the earlier chapters, the author has very judiciously determined the evolution of religions in the past under the aspect of their objectivity, he appears unable to disengage himself from a subjective altitude in his forecast of their future. Moreover, he has certainly neither been desirous of winning over the sympathies of contemporaries nor of recognising the power of modern thought when he writes of science that she is, when isolated from religion, a ' purveyor of pessimism.' "—*La Flandre Libérale*.

" M. de Molinari is a thorough Liberal and a sound Free Trader, and has at heart the best interests of France. . . . We can recommend those who would like to see the case for disestablishment stated in its widest bearings, and in a forcible and original manner, to read M. de Molinari's book for themselves."—Mr. W. Lloyd in the *Westminster Review*.

"Perhaps the general criticism would be that M. de Molinari feels the immense need of a religious appeal to move the masses of men, and would point his countrymen to Christianity as the highest religion, and the one ready in hand ; but when he comes to expound this faith, he speaks as one who has studied it from without, and that is a treatment of which Christianity, among all branches of study, is least susceptible."—Rev. J. O. Nash, in the *Economic Review*.

Printed by Cowan & Co., Limited, Perth.

www.ingramcontent.com/pod-product-compliance
Lightning Source LLC
Chambersburg PA
CBHW030826270326
41928CB00007B/908